The History of the Georgetown Evangelical Free Church

The History of the Georgetown Evangelical Free Church

Glynda Joy Nord

Order this book online at www.trafford.com
or email orders@trafford.com

Most Trafford titles are also available at major online book retailers.

Printed in the United States of America.

ISBN: 978-1-4669-0763-8 (sc)
ISBN: 978-1-4669-0764-5 (e)

Trafford rev. 02/10/2012

Trafford PUBLISHING www.trafford.com

North America & international
toll-free: 1 888 232 4444 (USA & Canada)
phone: 250 383 6864 • fax: 812 355 4082

CONTENTS

Dedication

To Richard, my devoted husband.
To Wesley and Anna Nord, my blessed in-laws.
To Lance, Letra and Clayton, my precious children.

Acknowledgements

My thanks to the many people who contributed to the writing of this book: Angeline Cassens, my sister-in-law, for allowing me to pick her brain about the smorgasbords, harvest festivals and confirmation classes; Carvin Youngbloom for the use of his *Swedes in Texas* book (English edition) and his contacts with former pastors and their families; Charlie Johnson for the use of his *Golden Jubilee, Swedish Free Church of the U.S.A.* book; Reverend David Gauthier for allowing me to have access to old church records; former church members for their reflections of days gone by for the "I Remember When" chapter; to friends, family, and church members that submitted recipes; Frieda Ryden Davidson and Ryden, Inc., for the design of the book's cover, which the church once used as the front cover for the Sunday bulletin; and last but not least, my critique partners, Dede Harper, Vivian Kirkbride, Joan Upton Hall, D.C. Campbell, Sylvia Dickey Smith, and Marcia Spillers. Without them, this manuscript would still be a work in progress.

God of Our Yesterday's
By
Matt Redman

We praise You-the God of our yesterdays
We praise You-the God who is here today
We praise You-our God, as tomorrow comes
We thank You-for grace in our yesterdays
We thank You-for peace in our hearts today
We thank You-our joy, as tomorrow comes
We will trust You, God! Amen
(chorus)

INTRODUCTION

Dear Readers,

The 120th Anniversary of the Georgetown Evangelical Free Church is first and foremost a celebration of God's grace and mercy demonstrated through generations of very real people, just like you and me. This is a story of courage, strength, determination and, most of all, faith.

It started when a small group of Swedish immigrants set out from their homeland facing a difficult journey to cross the Atlantic Ocean to an unknown land. Although they had sponsors, who were already in Texas, the courage they demonstrated in refusing to compromise their religious beliefs in the Word of God was "gospel" in their Scandinavian heritage. The strength and determination to maintain their identity and customs should be revered by all who benefit from their sacrifices.

The Georgetown Evangelical Free Church was integral to the growth of the Bell Community located five miles southeast of Georgetown in Williamson County, Texas. The church and the school were the focal points of this community which, in the early days, were impossible to separate from each other.

In this book, I weave together words and pictures of the church's history, with a glimpse into the lives of the earliest members, statements from former pastors, and reflections of yesteryear contributions collected from past and present members. I have also included some of the famous Swedish recipes that were made by the ladies of the church.

Even in the twenty-first century, by God's grace, there still remains courage, strength, determination and, most of all, *faith* in and among the people who currently make up the Georgetown Evangelical Free Church.

It has been a privilege for me to collect what information I could and document it for this very special time in history. It is also a blessing to know that my husband's ancestors, although not charter members, and our family has been a part of this history.

Sincerely,
Glynda Joy Nord

History of the Evangelical Free Church of America

The Evangelical Free Church of America observed its 125th Anniversary across the United States and Canada in 2009. This celebration was to *rejoice* in the goodness of God; the grace of our Lord Jesus Christ and the gifts of the Holy Spirit to the Church. To *respect* the faith of our fathers; the fruitful labors of our past and present leaders and the significances of missionary work at home and abroad. To *recognize* the heritage of sound doctrine; the need for Christian fellowship and the promise of Christ's Second Advent.

The Evangelical Free Church of America was formed by the association of two church bodies, the Swedish Evangelical Free Church, which had 185 congregations, and the Norwegian-Danish Evangelical Free Church Association with ninety churches. This merger took place in at a conference in June 1950 at the Medicine Lake Conference Grounds near Minneapolis, Minnesota. Both the international and national offices of the EFCA have been located in Minneapolis since the merger.

The Swedish church dates its formal beginnings to a conference held in Boone, Iowa in October 1884 when approximately twenty-seven churches joined forces to unite under one accord.

The Norwegian-Danish church was established by two churches in 1884: one in Tacoma, Washington and the other in Boston, Massachusetts. However, their national organization was not incorporated until 1912.

Over the past 125 plus years, The Evangelical Free Church of America has grown from 275 churches to nearly 1,500 autonomous churches united by a mutual commitment to serve our Lord Jesus Christ with the guidance of the Holy Spirit and the obedience to the Word of God. The organization is committed to cooperate with one another in ministry and fellowship as it seeks to fulfill the Great Commission which Christ has entrusted to His Church. The EFCA's growing ministry currently serves forty-five countries.

What does "Evangelical" mean?

The term *Evangelical* refers to the church's commitment to the proclamation of the Gospel and to the authority of Scripture as being inerrant in the original writings and the only safe and sufficient guide to faith and practice.

What does "Free" mean?

The term *Free* refers to the church's form of government as being congregational. To fully understand its significance, it is important to view the history from the perspective of the Swedish immigrants who brought with them the memory of the Lutheran church to America. In Sweden the Lutheran church was supported by the state through taxation of the people. Until about 1850, it was illegal for believers to hold religious meetings in their homes, to serve communion there, or to read the Bible. The pastors and other church officials were part of the power structure which, together with the nobles, law enforcement authorities, and the large landowners controlled their communities. When believers were permitted to worship freely, they referred to their assembled group as "free" congregations (free from state control). However "free" is a generic term and was applied to other denominations such as Baptists, Methodists, Mormons, etc.

EFCA STATEMENT OF FAITH

Adopted by the June 26, 2008 Conference

The Evangelical Free Church of America is an association of autonomous churches united around these theological convictions:

God

We believe in one God, Creator of all things, holy, infinitely perfect, and eternally existing in a loving unity of three equally divine Persons: the Father, the Son, and the Holy Spirit. Having limitless knowledge and sovereign power, God has graciously from eternity to redeem a people for Himself and to make all things new for His own glory.

The Bible

We believe that God had spoken in the Scriptures, both Old and New Testament, through the words of human authors. As the verbally inspired Word of God, the Bible is without error in the original writings, the complete revelation of His will for salvation, and the ultimate authority by which every realm of human knowledge and endeavor should be judged. Therefore, it is to be believed in all that it teaches, obeyed in all that it requires, and trusted in all that it promises.

The Human Condition

We believe that God created Adam and Eve in His image, but they sinned when tempted by Satan. In union with Adam, human beings are sinners by nature and by choice, alienated from God, and under His wrath. Only through God's saving work in Jesus Christ can we be rescued, reconciled, and renewed.

Jesus Christ

We believe that Jesus Christ is God incarnated, fully God and fully man, one Person in two natures. Jesus—Israel's promised Messiah—was conceived through the Holy Spirit and born of the virgin Mary. He lived a sinless life, was crucified under Pontius Pilate, arose bodily from the dead, ascended into heaven and sits at the right hand of God the Father as our High Priest and Advocate.

The Work of Christ

We believe that Jesus Christ, as our representative and substitute, shed His blood on the cross as the perfect, all-sufficient sacrifice for our sins. His atoning death and victorious resurrection constitute the only ground for salvation.

The Holy Spirit

We believe that the Holy Spirit, in all that He does, glorifies the Lord Jesus Christ. He convicts the world of its guilt. He regenerates sinners, and in Him they are baptized into union with Christ and adopted as heirs in the family of God. He also indwells, illuminates, guides, equips, and empowers believers for Christ-like living and service.

The Church

We believe that the true church comprises all who have been justified by God's grace through faith alone in Christ alone. They are united by the Holy Spirit in the body of Christ, of which He is the Head. The true church is manifest in local churches, whose membership should be composed only of believers. The Lord Jesus mandated two ordinances, baptism and the Lord's Supper, which visibly and tangibly express the gospel. Though they are not the means of salvation, when celebrated by the church in genuine faith, these ordinances confirm and nourish the believer.

Christian Living

We believe that God's justifying grace must not be separated from His sanctifying power and purpose. God commands us to love Him supremely and others sacrificially, and to live out our faith with care for one another, compassion toward the poor and justice for the oppressed. With God's Word, the Spirit's power, and fervent prayer in Christ's name, we are to combat the spiritual forces of evil. In obedience to Christ's commission, we are to make disciples among all people, always bearing witness to the gospel in word and deed.

Christ's Return

We believe in the personal, bodily, and pre-millennial return of our Lord Jesus Christ. The coming of Christ, at as time known only to God, demands constant expectancy and, as our blessed hope, motivates the believer to godly living, sacrificial service, and energetic mission.

Response and Eternal Destiny

We believe that God commands everyone everywhere to believe the gospel by turning to Him in repentance and receiving the Lord Jesus Christ. We believe that God will raise the dead bodily and judge the world, assigning the unbeliever to condemnation and eternal conscious punishment and the believer to eternal blessedness and joy with the Lord in the new heaven and the new earth, to the praise of His glorious grace. Amen.

Family of Faith

What We're About

Worship

We desire to grow in our devotion to Jesus Christ our Lord, both in our personal lives and when we gather together.

Instruction

We highly value the study of God's Word The Bible. It is our source of truth and authority for daily life.

Fellowship

We understand the church to be much like a family. Bonds of love and friendship are encouraged and cultivated here.

Evangelism

We have a precious message of hope and forgiveness to share with our community, city, state, nation, and world. It is the message of the cross and the empty tomb of Jesus Christ.

Who We Are

We're a Historical Church

The Georgetown Evangelical Free Church has the distinction of being the oldest Evangelical Free Church in the state of Texas. Founded in 1891, GEFC has maintained its rich heritage throughout the years while looking to embrace future generations.

We're a Family-sized Church

GEFC enjoys the advantages of a cozy sized congregation. There is a closeness here that feels like family, with people of all age groups represented.

We're a Friendly Church

The faithful folks who call GEFC their home know how to make visitors feel welcome. We have a warm, accepting character about us that is contagious.

We're a Hopeful Church

We're excited about our opportunities for the future. If you're looking for a church to call home, where you feel loved and have a motivation to be used of God, then consider joining us.

Where We're Going

We are on our way up! Our greatest desire it to please God and to obey His Word. Though we are small in size, we know that God can greatly use us in following His will.

We have great potential at our church for expanding ministries and creating new ones as the Lord brings gifted and willing people our way.

We desire to impact Georgetown with the Good News of eternal life in Christ and all that this new life has to offer. The great treasure we have is meant to be shared!

Historical Sketch of the Georgetown Evangelical Free Church

The Foundation

"Kindred spirits were soon knit together in mutual Christian love thus forming a small nuclei for more established Christian work in a later period. It was just such a group of believers that we find meeting regularly in various homes . . . for mutual spiritual edification through Bible study, testimony, and prayer." *Texas Posten*, July 2, 1981

In the fall of 1884, four young Swedes, Oscar Johnson, Carl Oscar Youngbloom, Ed Frezen, and Christina Forsvall arrived in Williamson County, Texas from the region of Jonkoping, Smaland, Sweden. They found work and settled throughout the area.

The following summer on one Sunday afternoon the three men, along with several other young adults, gathered in the home of Miss Forsvall who resided in Georgetown. There they studied God's word, and praised Him through songs and through prayer. That same day, Oscar Johnson and Carl Youngbloom made testimonies of the faith. Since their conversion, these Christians believed in the Free Church principles. This meeting was the start of the Evangelical Free Church movement across Texas.

Afterwards, the young people met often in Miss Forsvall's home to study the Bible and sing hymns. In these early gatherings, they also commemorated the death of Jesus by gathering around the Lord's Table.

Throughout the first few years of their worship services, itinerant evangelists often visited the group. In the spring and summer of 1888, Reverend C.V. Peterson, a circuit rider came to Texas to preach God's word. The following spring he returned bringing with him Reverend Edward Thorell. Later Reverend Nels Saabye arrived. Through His servants, God blessed the group and many souls were converted. The group began to grow, and meetings were held regularly in the homes of August Sandberg, Sven Peterson, S.A. Johnson and in others around the countryside.

Consequently in 1891, worshipers decided to officially organize a church. They met in the home of Sven Peterson to adopt a constitution and elect officers. The twenty-three charter members were: Carl Oscar Youngbloom, Johannes Julius Lawson, Mr. and Mrs. Hans Bostrom, Mr. and Mrs. J. August Sandberg, Mr. and Mrs. S.A. Johnson, Mr. and Mrs. Carl Edward Anderson, Mr. and Mrs. Carl Bjork, Mr. and Mrs. Sven Peterson, Erik Johan Brogren, Carl H. Gustafson, Gustaf F. Johnson, Mr. and Mrs. Carl Anderson, Mr. and Mrs. John Lax, and Mr. and Mrs. J.A. Eklund. The officers elected were: Carl Youngbloom, chairman (he held that position almost continuously until the time of his death in 1935); Hans Bostrom, secretary; and Johannes Lawson, treasurer (he also held his position for many years). The important office of elder was efficiently and faithfully filled by Carl H. Gustafson until the Lord called him home in 1932. On July 7, 1891 the group legally incorporated the first Swedish Evangelical Free Church in Texas according to the laws of the state—familiarly known as the Brushy Evangelical Free Church.

Footnote: The Texas Historical Marker states that twenty-one charter members gathered at Sven Peterson's home, which is correct, but there are twenty-three people listed in the church records as charter members.

The Mission House

"Take heed now; for the Lord hath chosen thee to build a house for the sanctuary: be strong, and do it." I Chronicles 28:10

Shortly after the church was erected, Reverend C.O. Sahlstrom, who traveled throughout Texas to other "Free" congregations such as Decker and Kimbro, held services for the group between 1891 and 1892. Through Sahlstrom's faithful ministry, a real old-fashioned revival started. Within a year the group of worshipers had grown so large that homes were no longer adequate to accommodate them.

Fortunately, at the time of founding, Mr. Charley J. Gustafson donated one and a half acres for a church building, or mission house as it was then called. This property was not good farmland but ideal for a church since it was on a hill visible from a distance. The location was five miles southeast of Georgetown near the intersection of the present County Roads 110 and 111. The site, now known as the Bell Gin area, was named after Calvin Bell who settled there in 1853. He and his fellow countrymen had a deep interest in their religious beliefs and the education of their children. By 1884, after the Bell School had already been built, the small Swedish community looked forward to adding a church.

Immediately members started to raise funds to build a House of Worship. In the summer of 1892 the "Mission House" (*missionshuset*) was started and completed in the fall at a cost of $650. All of the labor for construction was donated. A spirit of love, sacrifice, and zeal manifested. God and His work came first.

During the first years of activity, the congregation was unable to support a fulltime pastor. However this did not discourage worshipers, as regular meetings were held by some of the older or younger talented members such as Gustaf F. Johnson, who read and spoke of God's word. The church had visits from numerous preachers and missionaries as well.

In the early days of the church, no Sunday school activities took place because the children were too young. But within three years (by 1894), a children's class and an adult Bible class were formed with Mr. Carl H. Gustafson as the superintendent.

In the summer of 1896, once again the Lord visited this community and church with a mighty revival. The human instruments God used were Reverend Gustaf F. Johnson, who had recently returned from Japan, and Reverend John Herner. The Word was preached with the sharpness and power of the Holy Spirit and the old "*lasare*" songs, and other hymns such as *Children of the Heavenly Father*, were sung with vigor and warmth.

In 1897, a newly organized choir brought enthusiasm to the church, and the congregation employed its first minister, Reverend Alex Klint. He served for only a few months, but returned in 1903. He was the first pastor to teach a confirmation class. Eleven girls and seven boys attended, and the students graduated in 1904.

Over the next several years, Reverends Gustaf F. Johnson, August Modig, and William Nelson filled the pulpit, resulting in glorious revivals, and an increase in membership. Although the church had a high turnover of leaders, the congregation experienced steady and healthy growth and development.

Reverend Carl G. Athell assumed the leadership of the congregation in 1905 and continued for the next three years. Under his guidance, the church not only grew in membership but in other ways as well. The church facilities were enlarged to accommodate the growing Sunday school. The women formed the Ladies' Aid Society that helped and supported the needs of members, missionary work, and other good deeds. During this time a branch of the Sunday school was also organized in the Berry Springs Community (the Swedes called it Berry's). Pastor Athell taught two confirmation classes. The class of 1906 had ten girls and six boys confirmed, and the class of 1908 had nine girls and four boys confirmed. He also helped organize the adult choir.

When Pastor Athell made a trip to Sweden in 1907, Reverend E. Cederberg served as temporary pastor. He organized the Young People's Society which began with thirty charter members called "The Army of Hope." Through God's guidance, Cederberg continued to hold the young people's group together. He sought their interest and instructed them in the ways of the Father. Such great ministries required more space, so Mr. Gustafson added three and a half acres to the church's lot which made the property large enough for a parsonage to be built and the expansion of the cemetery.

In 1908, Reverend Carl J.E. Nelson received the call to lead the Swedish flock. During his ministry, the congregation decided to build a parsonage on the expanded land. Pastor Nelson taught the Confirmation Class of 1910 with twelve girls and eight boys confirmed. He served with great success for two years, but had to resign due to failing health in the spring after confirmation. Reverend Oscar Zahr ministered as temporary pastor for the reminder of the year. During his stay, the first summer camp meetings were held at Nelson Campground with the Reverend Morris Peterson as evangelist. This was another period of great revival and salvation, which resulted in further growth of the congregation.

In the beginning of January 1911, an energetic, cheerful young man from Michigan, Reverend H.A. Gustin, arrived to take over the pastoral duties of the church. Gustin had formerly ministered the Swedish Free

Church in Decker. He held the position there for two and a half years while at the same time was a student at Southwestern University in Georgetown. In addition to Gustin's everyday responsibilities with the church, he also held meetings in Jonah and Berry's Creek communities. He taught two confirmation classes: the class of 1912, with nine girls and nine boys, and the class of 1914, with thirteen girls and sixteen boys confirmed. The latter class was the largest in the history of the Brushy Evangelical Free Church.

In the fall of 1912, the young people from the Brushy Free Church invited other Free churches in Texas to a joint meeting or conference. Represented were Kimbro, Decker, Type, Elroy, Melvin, and the Epworth League of Georgetown. This was perhaps the first Y. P. Conference in the state. Throughout his faithful ministry, Pastor Gustin won the love and respect of those he shepherded; membership of the Brushy church had grown to over a hundred. Gustin served the Brushy church until March 1915. The next year he became Superintendant of the Christian Children's Home in Holdrege, Nebraska.

On Independence Day of 1915, Reverend E. H. Lindquist and his family arrived to take up the work of the church. While he labored here, the church continued to branch out into other communities. During his time, the church experienced remarkable inner strength and outer success, with a steady increase in membership as well as expanded activities. In December 1916, a small chapel was built in the Berry's Creek area and a Sunday school program was organized with Mr. Will Nord as superintendent. Sermons were delivered once a week for members and other Swedes, who resided in the area. Regular meetings continued to take place in Jonah as well. The Brushy church also enhanced their missionary vision to help with financial aid in the building of the Swedish Free Evangelical Church in Kenedy. While orchestrating missions, Pastor Lindquist still found time to conduct three confirmation classes: the class of 1917 had five girls and six boys; the class of 1918 had eight girls and one boy; and the class of 1920 had seven girls and eight boys confirmed.

In the summer of 1917, as American soldiers were sailing the Atlantic toward the battlefields of WWI, once again another series of tent meetings sparked revival within the congregation, and quite a number of people accepted Christ as their personal Savior.

By 1918 the Swedish Evangelical Free Church in Brushy had 110 adult members and the Sunday school had 130 pupils with youth classes counted as well. Including the Sunday school at Berry's Creek, there were a total of 155 pupils. And the Young People's Society had seventy-nine members. The total property value for both sites was $4,000.

In the fall of 1920 Reverend John Udd assumed the shepherd-hood. At this time, a sun porch was added to the parsonage, and plans for a new sanctuary were in the discussion stage. Mrs. Udd started the younger ladies group known as the "Earnest Workers" and Pastor Udd taught the Confirmation Class of 1922 with ten boys confirmed.

On January 1, 1923, the New Year began with the arrival of new church leadership, Reverend Alfred Stone and his family. During his ministry plans for a new church building was designed, and construction done in the spring and summer of the following year. Pastor Stone taught the Confirmation Class of 1924 with ten girls and six boys confirmed.

The organization grew steadily and continued to serve the needs of others through the changing times and circumstances. Besides community outreach, the congregation strongly supported missionary work in their homeland and in "heathen" areas. Several church members had left the church to spread the Word to other parts of the country. Gustaf F. Johnson became pastor in the Swedish Mission Tabernacle in Minneapolis. Ernest Johnson became pastor in the Swedish Evangelical Free Church in Keene, Nebraska. And F.O. Bergstrom, who also held sermons for the congregation, served more than twenty years in the mission field in Japan. Afterwards Bergstrom became a missionary in California where he preached in English, Swedish, and Japanese.

Cornerstones

"Now therefore ye are no more strangers and foreigners, but fellow citizens with the saints, and of the household of God. And are built upon the foundation of the apostles and prophets.
Jesus Christ himself being the chief corner stone. In whom all the building fitly framed together growth unto an holy temple in the Lord."

Ephesians 2:19-21

Within the first forty years of the Swedes arrival to their new homeland they heard of, and encountered, historical events that were taking place around them. Nationally, America had been involved in two wars, the

Spanish American (1894) and World War I (1917-1918). In 1901, the assassination of President William McKinley had shocked the world. In Texas, James Hogg the first native-born governor of Texas, took office in1891. The great Galveston hurricane of 1900 had destroyed immigration records of those who'd previously arrived. The gusher at "Spindletop" in 1901 created an interest in black gold. Closer to home, in Williamson County, the Friends of the Temperance League had played an active role between the late 1800s and early 1900s, which kept Georgetown, Round Rock, and Taylor dry towns. And the days of "pistol packin' preachers" had come and gone. The circuit riders who'd preached "fire and brimstone" were being replaced by pastors with families.

By 1924 the congregation of the Brushy Evangelical Free Church had outgrown the Mission House and plans were drafted for a new sanctuary. After the older structure had been dismantled on March 17th, the construction started on a more modern building with a seating capacity of about 300. The structure cost of just over $7,000 was dedicated entirely debt free four months later on July 13th. Like the old Mission House, the new church was built entirely with volunteer labor from its members. Years later Oscar Ekdahl said, "I have hammered a few nails in the old church."

Reverend Carl Malme was called to become the next pastor. He arrived in the spring of 1925 when the church experienced financial difficulties as a result of a severe drought that plagued Texas. The following year, to help increase finances on a regular basis, the church began an envelope system. This plan met with some success. All through those years of trials and tribulations the Lord continued to bless the Sunday school with new members. Malme taught two confirmation classes. The class of 1926 had four girls and four boys, and the class of 1930 had seven girls and five boys confirmed.

After Reverend Malme left in June of 1930, the church did not have a pastor until the spring of 1931 when Reverend Eric Frohman arrived with his family. The depression brought another financial pinch and a more permanent envelope system was introduced during his stay. The church came through this period quite successfully as the congregation continued its healthy growth. In the earlier years, all sermons were in Swedish, however, under Frohman's leadership, the Sunday morning worship service remained in Swedish and the evening worship service was conducted in

English. Pastor Frohman taught the Confirmation Class of 1933 with seven girls and two boys confirmed.

In August of 1934, Reverend Frohman left the Brushy church, and Reverend N. J. Christensen accepted the call as the new pastor. When he and his family arrived in September, the Lord kept them rooted longer than any previous pastors, six years. Due to the changes sweeping America, from rural to urban, the sons and daughters who were raised on farms departed for the city. With the congregation decline, Reverend Christensen was compelled to reach beyond the people with Swedish roots to everyone in the community. New avenues of communicating the Gospel were experienced during Christiansen's pastorate. With the aid of a public address system, he held street meetings from his car, and had a radio program that was broadcast from a Temple radio station. Christensen taught the Confirmation Class of 1935 with four girls and seven boys confirmed and the Confirmation Class of 1939 with eight girls and two boys confirmed. In January of 1940 Christiansen moved elsewhere. He returned a year later, along with Reverends Gustaf Johnson and Alfred Stone as speaker(s) at the church's Golden Jubilee.

The church was without a pastor for nearly seven months before Reverend Morris Rosene and family arrived in August. Under his shepherdhood the church broke away from the Swedish language and all services have been held in English ever since. Even the "*Jul Otta*," the traditional Christmas service was changed. By the time of the church's fiftieth anniversary in 1941, the congregation had grown to nearly 300 members and was the second largest Swedish Free Church in the state.

Rosene taught four confirmation classes; the most conducted by any single pastor of the church. The class of 1942 had five girls and five boys, the class of 1945 had seven girls and five boys; the class of 1948 had seven girls; and the class of 1951 had three girls and four boys confirmed.

Toward the end of Rosene's eleven-year-ministry at Brushy, the church purchased a portion of the old Bell School. It continued to operate until 1949, when students were transferred to Hutto, Georgetown, and Round Rock School Districts. The school was moved to the church's property and remodeled for a Christian educational and fellowship facility. Dedication services were held on July 3, 1951 during the church's Sixtieth Anniversary celebration. Other festivities that week were: Tuesday night was a fellowship banquet and the dedication of the chapel; Wednesday night was focused on the Women's Missionary Society, with the evangelistic service given by

Reverend Frohman; Thursday night was focused on the Sunday School, with the service given by Reverend Frohman; Friday night was focused on the Young People's Society, with service given by Reverend Frohman; Saturday night was the State F.C.Y. F. Conference Rally; and Sunday, Reverend N. J. Christianson gave the morning worship message, which was followed by the afternoon Jubilee Service given by Reverend Ernest Johnson, and the evening service given by Reverend Frohman.

Less than two weeks after the church's Sixtieth Anniversary, the congregation voted to change the church's name. The name "Evangelical Free Church of Georgetown" was taken instead of "Brushy Evangelical Free Church."

From August 1951 to May 1956, Reverend Arthur Anderson was the pastor of the church. In his first year, he led the men to organize the Brotherhood. The group composed of men in the church and community for Christian fellowship met bi-monthly to promote projects within the church, community, and district. The next year Reverend Anderson orchestrated the purchase of an organ for the music ministry of the church. He taught the Confirmation Class of 1954 with seven girls and four boys being confirmed.

Toward the end of the 1950s a number of major improvements were added to the church property, namely the installation of a butane gas system for both the church and the parsonage; the construction of a sun parlor to replace the old front porch on the parsonage; and the remodeling of the old bath room into a modern one.

As the Brushy Evangelical Free Church moved toward its seventieth anniversary, the congregation became aware of its decline in membership and Sunday school attendance. Much of the concern was due to a "rural-to-urban" shift. Changes needed to be made which caused the members to think about another location for its ministry.

Under the leadership of Reverend Bertil Thorne, who had arrived in April 1956, the congregation prayed for direction about the situation. Between 1930 to 1959, Williamson County experienced a large population decline. However, the City of Georgetown had nearly doubled in size during this period. The congregation began to lean toward moving to Georgetown. Thorne suggested the purchase of a lot at the corner of University Avenue and Hutto Road. After seeking God's guidance, the congregation bought the property on February 15, 1960. Two years later the congregation voted to build a new church on the lot as soon as finances would allow.

Meanwhile on July 5-9, 1961 the Evangelical Free Church of Georgetown celebrated its Seventieth Anniversary with nightly festivities. Former pastors were invited to speak: Reverend Carl J. E. Nelson, Reverend N. J. Christensen and Reverend Arthur E. Anderson. Special music was provided by the Elgin Free Church, Crestview Free Church (Austin), and First Free Church (Austin). A church banquet was held on Saturday night at the L&M Cafe in Georgetown.

Through much prayer, and believing that the move to Georgetown was God's will, on Easter Sunday, April 1963, a ground breaking ceremony took place on the previously purchased lot; construction of the third church building started, located at 1322 E. University Ave. Meanwhile, church members raised money for the purchase of pews, hymnals, Bibles, and other items needed for their new sanctuary. Several months later the new facilities were dedicated on September 8th and the "Evangelical Free Church of Georgetown" changed its name to the "Georgetown Evangelical Free Church."

According to Reverend Bertil Thorne the move was a real transition, as members still loved the old church. For over seventy years many sentiments were attached to both the church and the parsonage where weddings, anniversaries, holiday festivities, funerals, and other celebrations had taken place. But prior need to fulfill the church's role in the present day world had ordered the move. During Reverend Thorn's ministry, the church, once again, had a radio program ministry. He taught two confirmation classes. The class of 1957 had two girls and five boys confirmed, and the class of 1961 had two girls and three boys confirmed. In January 1965, Thorne completed his service in Georgetown; however he returned years later and was given the honored title of Pastor Emeritus from the Georgetown Evangelical Free Church.

When the congregation relocated to Georgetown, the old church building was sold and dismantled. The portion that was part of the old Bell School was bought by N.G. Whitlow. He moved the structure to Round Rock and converted into a warehouse behind the Round Rock Cemetery off Sam Bass Road. The parsonage was also sold, but remains on the original site. The cemetery, on the original tract of land, is still used for burials even today. Although the cemetery is owned by the church, it has an active association that was formed in the fall of 1978 for the purpose of maintaining the grounds and other needs.

Transition

"In spite of many mistakes and failures in our past, God has been faithful and good to us. Only by putting our little hand of faith in His mighty hand of power and letting Him guide us in the days to come, dare we face the future that looms up so dark and perilous in these last days. Our desire as a church is to remain a beacon light . . . sending out the rays of hope and warning of the Gospel until Jesus comes." *Texas Posten*, July 2, 1981

Over the last forty years, members of the Swedish Free Church had witnessed even more history and mayhem than their Sweden-born ancestors. The United States had been engaged in World War II, the Korean War, and the Vietnam War. The latter had caused a number of young men from the Georgetown Evangelical Free Church to enlist in the Armed Forces. Russia launched Sputnik. The tragic assassination of another United States President, John F. Kennedy, happened on Texas soil. And transportation by gasoline engines replaced the mule-drawn-wagon.

Although times were rapidly changing, the second and third generations of Swedish Americans still embraced their Christian heritage and traditions.

After Reverend Thorn left in January 1965, E. L. Pearson was the interim pastor until August. During this time the congregation voted to build a parsonage in Georgetown. The church purchased land and built a three bedroom brick home at 1806 Louise Street. When Reverend Walter Osborn arrived in September, the new parsonage was ready for occupancy. The church celebrated it's Diamond Anniversary (75 years) on July 7, 1966. Also during Reverend Osborn's two years of ministry, he conducted the Confirmation Class of 1967, all three children (two girls and one boy) were from the Herbert Ekvall family.

In October 1967, Reverend Richard Mittanck became pastor and served the church for five years. Having been saved through the Campus Crusade for Christ, his outreach to the unsaved was to spread the Gospel through various evangelism methods. During his ministry, Reverend

Aubrey McGann conducted two evangelistic crusades in which the Spirit touched the lives of several people.

Reverend Larry Larson labored as pastor from February 1973 through May 1975. His ministry touched the lives of several couples living in the Georgetown area. Some of them strengthened the church choir. Pioneer Girls, an outreach for young girls, was also instituted. Pastor Larson also taught the Confirmation Class of 1973 in which two boys were confirmed, the smallest class in the church's history.

From July 1976 to June 1982, Reverend Raymond J. Wegner served as pastor. During this time the small house next to the church, known as the "shack," was purchased and furnished for a nursery and used as Sunday school space. Today the building is still being used for the children's ministry. The mortgage on the parsonage was burned, and the note on the shack was paid in a short time. Several Vacation Bible Schools were held, as well as Easter and Christmas programs. The Women's Ministry met monthly and the annual mother/daughter banquet was held on Saturday night of Mother's Day weekend. Members with young families participated in a weekend camp out at Twin Oaks Ranch in Buda.

On July 7, 1981, the church celebrated its Ninetieth Anniversary Commemoration with Dr. Thomas McDill, EFCA president as speaker. Like the Seventieth Anniversary, festivities were held nightly for four nights with Dr. McDill as the only speaker. However special music given by Mrs. Hubert Ekvall and Mrs. Joyce Wegner, Red Team Chapel (Fort Hood), Trinity Free Church (Austin), and First Free Church (Austin).

One of Reverend Wegner's main ministries while pastor was community outreach to men and women via Bible studies in the church. Various Bible study groups emerged under the auspices of the church: ladies' morning, men's noon, couples' evening, and Southwestern University students. During this period in history, the congregation enjoyed a close relationship with Chaplain Gary Sanford and family from Fort Hood. They brought visitors to our Sunday evening services. The church encouraged fellowship and a time of sharing with the Fort Hood soldiers, which led the church supporting the Soldier's Hospitality House in Killeen. The church also supported the Faith Evangelical Free Church in Round Rock from its onset.

Pastor Wegner gave strong attention to Scripture with the spiritual focus being "Study the Book." In the course of his seven year service, he presented teaching from nearly all portions of the Bible.

Reverend Daryl V. Walling arrived in January 1983, after interim ministry by Pastor Bertil Thorn. Walling served the church until July 1988. His spiritual focus was on testimonies and witnessing. Several special meetings with outside speakers were held. Weekly prayer meetings were revamped, which met in the main sanctuary, with singing and a special sheet of prayer requests and study outlines were given at each meeting. He also taught the Confirmation Class of 1986 with three girls and two boys confirmed. A youth group was restarted, with parties and a quiz team, culminating in the Georgetown group of winning three trophies on district level. The church hosted the District Conference in which Ed and Socorro Woodbury were commissioned into missionary service in Zaire, Africa. Christmas programs directed by Mrs. Walling were especially memorable. The church parking lot was paved, for the first time. And Reverend Walling was directly involved in the organization of the Killeen Evangelical Free Church.

In October 1988 Reverend Gordon T. Bakan began his service as minister. The first major highlight of Bakan's ministry was the dedication and placement of the Texas State Historical Marker, located on the east side of the building, on March 19, 1989. Unfortunately the historical marker states twenty-one charter members instead of the twenty-three charter members (their names are listed in the Foundation section).

Pastor Bakan also founded the outreach program "The Phone's For You" and taught the Confirmation Class of 1992 with one girl and three boys confirmed. This was the last confirmation class of the Georgetown Free Church.

Church members that were fifty-five and older decided to form a Senior Citizens' Fellowship. They met bi-monthly on the third Tuesday for a potluck dinner in the back of the church. The group had many worthwhile projects.

In 1990 as members were planning for the church's centennial anniversary, U.S. troops had been deployed, once again, this time to Saudi Arabia. Operation Desert Storm was underway. Only one young man from the church joined the Armed Forces at this time; luckily, the war had ended before he finished Basic Training.

The church celebrated its One Hundredth Anniversary, July 7-14, 1991. Reverend Bertil Thorne started the week-long activities as speaker for the Sunday morning worship service. Karen Strand, Sylvia Carnes, and the church choir presented special music. Reverend Ken Wooten from the

Killeen Evangelical Free Church spoke at the evening service; the music was also provided by the Killeen church. In the evenings throughout the week, various speakers and special music were presented. On Saturday night, the Centennial Banquet was held with Dr. Paul Cedar, President of the Evangelical Free Church of America, as guest speaker; he also presided over the Sunday morning service. A special Centennial Anniversary Service took place on Sunday afternoon with Reverend George Walker, Superintendent, Northern Plains District of the Evangelical Free Church, as speaker. Special music was provided by Mrs. Joyce Wegner. Refreshments were served after the service. To commemorate the church's founding members the decorations were blue and yellow, Sweden's national colors.

After the church's anniversary, membership dropped to an all-time low, which was due to many reasons. When Pastor Bakan and his family left the church, the children's Sunday school ceased as there were no longer any children in attendance. The youngest couple, Richard and Joy Nord, were in their mid forties with grown children who worshiped elsewhere.

In December 1994, the church welcomed Reverend Tommy Rosenblad as their pastor. Unfortunately, one of his main duties were to conduct funerals just as the first and some second-generation descendants from the early members began to pass away. Beside preaching on Sunday morning, nursing home and hospital visits became his main focus in his Free Church ministry.

After Rosenblad left to further his education, the church called Reverend Lou Herman as pastor. However, due to uncontrollable circumstances, he only ministered three months before moving to Illinois. Before Herman's departure he informed the congregation, on the same Sunday he resigned, that sitting among them was a highly qualified individual who had recently graduated from Moody Bible Institute in Chicago—David Gauthier. Upon Herman's request, Reverend Gauthier preached his first sermon on September 20, 1998.

As the world prepared for the Millennium, Reverend Gauthier focused on how to revive a dying church. Membership had plunged to an all-time low. The average attendance for Sunday morning service was between fifteen to twenty worshipers, which was fewer attendees than when the church was erected one hundred and eight years prior. Since Pastor Herman had graciously served without pay, the question arose, "Could the church afford to pay its bills plus a full time pastor?" Rumors about disbanding and closing the church's doors forever, began to swarm like flies over a corpse. If Gauthier wanted to quit his "day job" he had work to do. Needless to say, the power of prayer and never-ending faith kept the doors open and the congregation offered Pastor Gauthier a salary.

With the arrival of the twenty-first century, many old traditions within the church changed. Society was setting a new trend in the dress code for attending church. Worshipers no longer wore their "Sunday best" as men's suits and ties, and women's dresses were replaced with casual wear like jeans and pullover shirts.

The praise and worship music also changed. Traditional hymns, accompanied by an organ or a piano, were slowly being altered with upbeat songs, which repeated the same words, and required band-style instruments. This "contemporary" music started to split the congregation, some people actually left to worship elsewhere. However, Reverend Gauthier tried to please everyone, and in hopes of drawing more worshipers, he held two Sunday morning services. The first had contemporary music and the second had traditional hymns. After a year of him preaching the same sermon twice, and with no substantial membership growth, the church returned to one service. Today the music is a blend of traditional hymns and contemporary songs which are accompanied by numerous guitars, a piano, and even drums.

Fortunately one thing didn't change within the church at the turn of the century, preaching God's Word. Even before the church was officially established in 1891, its founders were blessed with men who loved the Lord and preached the Scriptures. Pastor Gauthier has never faltered on that aspect; his sermons are taken directly from the Bible.

Through the years Gauthier has taught Sunday school, led adult mid-week Bible studies and prayer groups, offered one on one discipleship, and began an outreach ministry to the students at Southwestern University. He and his wife, Kristi, also organized children's festivals, kids movie outreach, and backyard Bible clubs for kids.

Since Pastor Gauthier owned his home, in 2005 the church's parsonage on Louise Street was sold. The money was applied to the purchase of the house at 1302 Hutto Road (across the parking lot from the church) to be used as the pastor's office and the adult Sunday school. Several years later the church brought the brown house next to the "shack" to be used for church related activities; however this violated the city's ordnance and the building was used for other purposes.

In 2010 a playground and fence was built to accommodate the needs of the children's ministry. That same year, and into the spring of 2011, the church building was renovated—the forty-seven year-old interior received a facelift. The pews were removed and replaced by padded chairs. The choir loft was dismantled, and the organ was sold. This made more room for the extended stage. The brown paneling was painted off white, which lightened-up the 1960s atmosphere, and the Florissant lights were replaced by modern track-lights. The inside now resembles that of a "start up church" which wasn't necessarily a bad concept considering there are only a handful of members related to those four young Swedes who first gathered in Miss Forsvall's home in 1884.

On November 13, 2011 the Georgetown Evangelical Free Church celebrated its One Hundred Twentieth Anniversary. Although the church had reached that milestone in July, the congregation decided to commemorate the event during the Thanksgiving season. The festivities included the morning worship service, followed by the noon meal, and a special program. Joyce Wegner and Lani Winstrom provided the music. Former pastors, Tommy Rosenblad and Ray Wegner participated in the program. And longtime-church-member, Charlie Johnson, treated the audience with *Children of the Heavenly Father,* which he sang in Swedish. At the end of the day, old and new acquaintances bid their farewells until the next celebration.

Reverend Gauthier stated, "This day was important because we were able to bring young and old, new and seasoned, near and far together for a celebratory moment of joyful Christian unity. However its greatest significance lay in the fact that we were given such a rich opportunity to pause and truly express our heart's gratitude and praise to the God who has brought us this far—with a bright shred hope for tomorrow."

CHURCH ORGANIZATIONS

Sunday School

In the fall 1894, church members recognized the importance of instructing their children in the Word of God and teaching them to trust and to follow the Good Shepherd. So they held a meeting to organize a Sunday school. The men in attendance, Carl H. Gustafson, Johannes J. Larson, Emil Lind, Carl O. Youngbloom and John Rosenblad, Sr., had a spirit of most earnest concern for God's work.

Mr. Gustafson, selected as the first superintendent of the Brushy Evangelical Free Church, was a young man of deep spiritual convictions and a holy devotion to God from the day of his conversion. He proposed two classes, one for the adults and the other for the children. Brother Larson taught the adult class and Brother Rosenblad taught the children's class. Some of the first children to attend Sunday school were Rebecca Johnson, Hilda and Dina Sandberg, and Selma, Mollie, and Dixie Bergstrom.

By 1901, there were five classes. On the first Sunday of the month, an offering was taken and the money went toward special projects such as helping the needy or purchasing items for the church. The missionary spirit of the Sunday school leaders prompted the church to start another Sunday school in 1907, this time in the Berry's Creek Community. Also beginning in 1907, and continuing for several years, Swedish language classes of a month's duration were conducted for the children. Attendance records were first kept in 1910. Nine classes were conducted in 1915, and a year later, there were twenty-five children enrolled with Will Nord as superintendent. The Brushy church had twelve Sunday school classes that year. A chapel was built at Berry's Creek in 1917 and later moved to Bell County.

Beginning in 1927 the English language was phased into the Sunday school classes. By 1933 enrollment between the two churches had risen to 178 pupils. Daily Vacation Bible School, which took place during the summer, started in 1942 and continued until the mid 1980s.

Missions had been implemented in the Sunday school by giving to the Children's Home in Nebraska, and various foreign missionaries. Also one year they gave Bibles to children in the community who had none.

During the holiday season another endeavor was the promotion of the first children's Christmas program. Although the knowledge and experience as to how to proceed with such a task was lacking, Reverend August Ohlson, an old-time preacher, who just happened to be in the area, helped and inspired with the project. The children sang songs and recited scripture or other material, known as their "piece," about the Savior's birth. The Christmas program was done annually for over a hundred years. After the program, everyone in attendance received an apple, and the children also received a bag of candy.

Throughout the years, the Sunday school enrollment has changed. The largest enrollment in Sunday school was in 1941. The eight classes and teachers served 150 pupils, an adult men's class, an adult women's class, and six other classes that provided Bible teachings for the youth and small children.

Today, even though the church has a small congregation, the desire for Sunday school continues to live and grew spiritually. Its mission is to serve as a beacon of light and be a channel of blessing for those who attend as they may learn what the Holy Bible teaches and be guided to Him who alone can give eternal life.

Women's Ministry

Just in time for the "season of giving" on December 5, 1905, the ladies of Brushy church met in the home of Mrs. Carl H. Johnson to organize the Ladies' Aid Society. Their purpose was to provide a time of spiritual edification and Christian fellowship for the women of the church. From the society's humble beginning, their work grew and prospered for more than a century. Although the organization's name has changed several times over the years, the mission has always been the same.

At the first gathering Mrs. Ida Anderson was elected chairman. She was a warm-hearted, true, and zealous worker and leader. During her leadership, the society grew spiritually and new members were welcomed. She held office for twenty-two years until the Lord called her home on the day of the August meeting of 1927. The other officers elected at the first meeting were Miss Ellen Anderson (Ida's daughter), secretary and Miss Ruth Larson, treasurer. During a later meeting, Mrs. August Peterson, also a zealous and true-hearted leader, was elected vice-chairman.

Reverend Carl Athell, the pastor at the time of organization, was very interested in this new branch of church service and took an active part in every meeting. Since then most pastors have also supported the women's groups either by giving spiritual talks or by financial backing via the church board.

In January 1921, under the influence of Mrs. John Udd, the Earnest Workers, a ladies group for young women, was organized. The first meeting was held at the home of Mrs. Royal Ryden at which time the election of officers took place. Mrs. Udd, the pastor's wife, became its first chairman. She held the office faithfully and efficiently until she and her husband moved. Minnie Johnson was elected vice-chairman; Mrs. C.T. Anderson, secretary; Mrs. Royal Ryden, vice-secretary; and Alma Carlson, treasurer. At this time, the following ladies also joined thus making them charter members: Minnie Johnson, Ruth Anderson, Mabel Lax, Ester Anderson, Naomie Gustafson, Mrs. Will Ryden, Alma Anderson, Nora Johnson, Lizzie Anderson, Annie Gustafson, Beda Johnson, Hannah Anderson, Mrs. Wesley Youngbloom, and Mrs. Walter Johnson.

Meetings were held monthly throughout the twenty years of existence and were well attended. The organization was very active in helping the church in many areas besides carrying on missionary work both at home and abroad. During the earlier years, sewing was done at each meeting.

Between meetings, the women would also sew at home to prepare for the annual bazaar held in the fall. The proceeds went toward the building fund and other projects. In the later years varied devotional programs were presented and membership dues were collected.

The following figures might give some indication of the organizations activities. A total of $4,609 was taken in over the years. Cash donations for the new church building was $2,030; gifts for upkeep and different articles for the church and parsonage $413; support of missions, Children's Home in Holdrege and to the Women's Missionary Society, $368 while $1,797 was kept in the treasury to buy needed supplies to carry on His work.

After twenty years, the Earnest Workers realized that they were no longer young women and therefore merged with the Ladies' Aid Society.

Over the years the women of the church became involved in various foreign and home mission projects and filled an important place in the work of their own church. Today, the women's ministry neither has a formal name, nor membership, nor officers. However, the ladies still support ministries such as the Williamson County Pregnancy Help Center, Samaritan's Purse, and the Soldier's Hospitality House near Fort Hood. With grateful hearts to our Heavenly Father, we remember the blessings of the past and pledge ourselves to greater loyalty to the cause of our Lord and Savior.

A group of thirty young people, under the leadership of Reverend Edwin Cederberg gathered at the Brushy "Mission House" on July 23, 1907 to organize the Young People's Society. During that meeting the name "Hoppets Har" was decided upon, which translates to "The Army of Hope." The first board members were: Oscar Johnson, chairman; Axel Anderson, vice-chairman; Agnes Carlson, secretary; and Philip Carlson, treasure. That evening a constitution was put before the house and was accepted with only minor changes. Twenty-seven years later, most of the rules and bylaws were still being used when the name was changed to the "Young People's Society."

The high point of the society's existence was on April 20, 1912 with a statewide conference held at the Brushy Free Church. Youths from Kimbro, Decker, Type, Melvin, Elroy, and the Epworth League of Georgetown were invited to attend.

Different reports indicate that the Young People's Society contributed numerous gifts to the church such as books for the church library, two sets of song books, Bibles, furniture for the parsonage, monies toward a piano and an organ, etc. Besides financial help to the church, the society gave a number of donations to several missionaries, a Bible School in Nebraska, as well to the Swedish Sanitarium in Colorado.

For over seventy years the aim for the organization had always been to unite the young people of the community in Christian fellowship. The programs were made up of Bible studies, songs, prayers, and declamations. Due to the lack of young people, this organization no longer exists. However through God's love and mercy, may He sustain and keep us so our welcoming arms shall always be extended to youthful Christians so that this ministry can exist once again.

Men's Brotherhood

In 1951 Reverend Arthur Anderson led the men to organize the Brotherhood as an avenue of fellowship in the community. The group met bi-monthly and was composed of men in the church and community for Christian fellowship and promotion of projects within the church, community, and district.

Although the Brotherhood has not always been a continuous ministry, today the men meet monthly for breakfast to study the Word and help with improvements around the church and other properties owned by the Free Church.

Choir

Worshipers sometimes sang as a group even as far back as when Alex Klint was pastor in 1903. But it was not until Carl G. Athell's ministry two years later that a regular choir was started. From that time until the mid 1980s the choir continued its ministry of song with few intermissions. The various pastors or pastors' wives were generally the choir directors. Local talent was also used such as Edwin Anderson and Bertha Bowman.

The young people thought that organizing a Junior Choir would be helping the church as well as themselves. Therefore a choir was organized in the spring of 1940. The following were chosen as officers: Hannah Anderson, director; Irene Lindquist, pianist; and Waldine Carlson, secretary. Practice was held on Friday evenings. The choir rendered their singing at either the Sunday morning service or the Sunday evening service. Upon the arrival of Reverend Rosene, a short Bible study was held immediately after the practice.

Even though music is an important part of the congregation's worship, the church has not had a choir since the mid 1980s. This was mainly due to the dwindling of church membership.

Confirmation Class

Reverend Alex Klint began the first Bible instruction course, known as confirmation class, in 1903. Students entering the seventh grade, or between twelve and thirteen years, would attend confirmation classes. The purpose was to help students learn how to study the Bible, learn the meaning of the scriptures, memorize scripture, and to acquire information about the doctrine of the Evangelical Free Church. Classes were usually held on Saturday afternoons for several hours during the school year. Depending on special circumstances, however, sometimes the classes lasted longer.

Once the classes were complete, Confirmation Sunday arrived. Students proceeded into the church and sat in the choir area facing the congregation. Students were questioned by the pastor about their knowledge of the Bible, and verses were recited. Each student received a confirmation certificate and a new Bible as a gift from the church.

It was customary for the boys to wear dark suits and the girls to wear white dresses. For this occasion, a photographer was hired to record the special day with a formal class picture. Some class members would also commemorate this day with an individual photograph.

Confirmation Class of 1904
Ester Burk, Agnes Carlson, Ellen Anderson, Ruth Lawson, Hulda Lax, Ellen Anderson, Ida Burk,
Esther Anderson, Ellen Engvall, Anna Lax, Eric Strand, John Anderson, Edwin Anderson, Eric Carlson,
Tom Anderson, Wesley Youngbloom, Frank Mercer, (one unidentified) Rev. Alex Klint

Confirmation Class of 1906
Eric Lax, Ben Lawson, Henry Lax, Reuben Lawson, Carl Anderson, Philip Youngbloom,
Ruth Peterson, Edith Peterson, Esther Carlson, Alma Carlson, Annie Strand, Edith Strand, Ruth Burk,
Ellen Nord, Birdie Lawson, Annie Gustafson, Rev. Carl Athell

Confirmation Class of 1908
John Anderson, Edith Carlson, Gertrude Dahlberg, Hilding Bergstrom,
Bessie Bergstrom, Rose Bergstrom, Annie Anderson, Rose Anderson, Maud Carlson,
Philip Bergstrom, Ruth Ahlberg, Hulda Anderson, Gustaf Peterson, Rev. Carl Athell

Confirmation Class of 1910
Oscar Gustafson, Alice Anderson, Clarence Peterson, Rosa Youngbloom, George Youngbloom, Rose Engvall, Oscar Nord, Esther Peterson, Oscar Holmstrom, Gus Bergstrom, Hilde Bergstrom, Minnie Johnson, Rev. Carl Nelson, Nellie Gustafson, Alma Wohlander, Fred Anderson, Rhoda Rosenblad, Annie Gustafson, Hulda Peterson, Beda Johnson, C.T. Anderson

Confirmation Class of 1912
Signe Wolander, Gunner Ekdahl, Naomi Gustafson, Signe Anderson, Mabel Peterson, Paul Eklund, Simon Peterson, Alda Anderson, Julius Lawson, Ruth Anderson, Esther Anderson, Joe Rosenblad, Mabel Lax, Naomi Gustafson, Frank Carlson, Minnie Eklund, Leonard Carlson, Eric Swenson, Rev. H.A. Gustin

Confirmation Class of 1914
C.H. Johnson, Ben Rosenblad, Arthur Lax, Joe Bergstrom, Eliott Brogren, Joseph Johnson, Gus Johnson, Elmer Nord, Oscar Ekdahl, Enoch Anderson, John Hallman, Reuben Peterson, Arvid Lindelius, Carl Lindelius, John Gustafson, Hadley Nord, Rosa Nord, Elizabeth Anderson, Mabel Gilberg, Mildred Mercer, Nora Johnson, Ester Nord, Elna Younghloom, Ellen Gustafson, Alma Anderson, Naomi Younghloom, Agda Anderson, Mabel Wohlander, Alice Gustafson, Rev. H.A. Gustin

Confirmation Class of 1917
Reuben Rosenblad, Arnold Peterson, Emil Ekdahl, Reuben Anderson, Martin Bergstrom, Lawerence Gilberg, Alma Anderson, Alda Nord, Rev. E.H. Lindquist, Edna Anderson, Naomi Nord, Hannah Anderson

Confirmation Class of 1918
Mina Anderson, Lillie Anderson, Nora Johnson, Naomi Nord
Ellen Begstron, Edith Lax, Rev. E.H. Lindquist, Elvina Johnson, Elmer Bowman

Confirmation Class of 1920
Roland Anderson, Tom Rosenblad, Arnold Lindquist, Oscar Anderson, Philip Fosberg
Mildred Anderson, Martin Nord, Sigurd Johnson, Oscar Carlson, Anna Bergstrom
Ethel Carlson, Evelyn Carlson, Rev. E.H. Lindquist, Bertha Bowman, Ethel Nord, Florence Nord

Confirmation Class of 1922
Joe Peterson, Weldon Lindquist, Wesley Johnson, Wesley Ekdahl, Oscar Bergstrom, John Rosenblad, Arthur Anderson, Paul T. Anderson, Rev. John Udd, Oscar C. Anderson, Paul Bowman

Confirmation Class of 1924
Lillian Nord, Wesley Nord, Alford Peterson, Martin Johnson, Roy Bowman, Lillian Anderson, Irene Johnson, Elizabeth Nord, Lillie Nord, Rev. Alfred Stone, Martha Anderson, Mildred Ekdahl, Martha Anderson, Howard Lindquist, Lawrence Rosenblad, Edna Carlson, Deborah Bowman

Confirmation Class of 1926
Morris Johnson, Mildred Anderson, Edna Lind, Howard Anderson,
Roy Carlson, Ethel Anderson, Rev. C.A. Malme, Gladys Youngbloom, Bertil Bowman

Confirmation Class of 1930
Evelyn Anderson, Juliet Ekdahl, Howard Carlson, Ora May Youngbloom, Annabel Peterson,
Jeannette Carlson Loraine Anderson, George Carlson, Roland Anderson, Rev. C.A. Malme, Homer
Anderson, Oliver Anderson, Marian Malme

Confirmation Class of 1933
Irene Anderson, Rev. Eric Frohman, Frances Anderson, Franklin Anderson, Helen Carlson,
Harry Anderson, Irene Lindquist, Vivian Anderson, Ruth Carlson, Ruby Lee Anderson

Confirmation Class of 1935
Standley Anderson, Charles Ryden, Irving Borg, Beatrice Carlson,
Marshall Anderson, Bernice Anderson, Elmer Anderson,
Benton Carlson, Pauline Anderson, Rev. N.J. Christensen, LaVerne Anderson, Earl Ryden

Confirmation Class of 1939
Marjorie Youngbloom, Edith Carlson, Ruby Nell Anderson, Grace Christensen,
Clarice Anderson, Waldine Carlson, Marvin Anderson, Annie Marie Anderson,
Rev. N.J. Christensen, Rachel Peterson, Virgil Carlson

Confirmation Class of 1942
Doris Anderson, Pauline Rosene, Iris Anderson, Sylvia Peterson, Viola Nord, Dorothy Nord
Herbert Anderson, Lee Roy Nord, Rev. Morris Rosene, Carl Wilbert Johnson, Everett Ryden

Confirmation Class of 1945
Imogene Johnson, Dorothy Lewis, Vernon Eklund, Ruth Lewis, Rhonda Ann Ryden,
Doris Nord, Betty Jane Nord, Tillman Johnson,Charles Johnson, Rev. Morris Rosene,
Earl Carlson, Reuben Nord Jr., Arnell Youngbloom

Confirmation Class of 1948

Grace Ekdahl, Joyce Minzenmeyer, Irene Minzenmeyer, Mary Ann Jacobson, Elaine Rosenblad,
Jackie Liardon, Mavis Rosene, Rev. Morris Rosene

Confirmation Class of 1951
Angeline Nord, Caroline Joyce Anderson, Natalie Rosenblad, Myrten Lindon,
Curtis Nord, Rev. Morris Rosene, Barto Patterson, Clayton Johnson

Confirmation Class 1957
Jerry Forberg, Darrell Ekdahl, Richard Oman, Richard Nord,
Neal Anderson, Rev. Bertil Thorne, Katherine Nord, Sylvia Thorne

Confirmation Class of 1954
Kathy Anderson, James Murphy, Enid Anderson, Rev. Arthur Anderson,
Lyndon Rosenblad, Barbara Anderson, Rosalie Anderson, David Oman, Ruth Johnson,
Bernice Nord, Joan Rosenblad, Carvin Youngbloom

Confirmation Class of 1961
Sammy Liardon, Gary Payne, Robert Payne, Linda Ekdahl.

Confirmation Class of 1967
Norma Ekvall, Richard Ekvall, Helen Ekvall, Rev. Walter Osborn

Confirmation Class of 1973
Bradley Larson, Rev. Larry Larson, Truman Johnson

Confirmation Class 1986
Michael Walling, Lance Nord, Mary Robbins, Becky Wegner, Ann Wegner

Confirmation Class of 1992
Rev. Bertil Thorne, Rev. Gordon Bakan, Brian Powell, Clayton Nord, Mark Wegner, Teresa Wegner

The Cemetery

On July 7, 1891, the first Evangelical Free Church in Texas was incorporated, according to the laws of the state, with twenty three charter members. Less than a month later Mr. Charley J. Gustafson donated to the church one and a half acres of land, which started at the southwest corner of a 125 acre L shaped tract, to the newly formed "Free Swedish Evangelical Church". Even though Mr. Gustafson did not worship with his fellow Swedes there, he felt compelled to deed the property to them, especially since it was not profitable farmland. Actually he sold it to them for one dollar. On February 11, 1907, Mr. Gustafson once again deeded (for the price of one dollar) an additional three and a half acres to the church, bringing the total landholdings to five acres, which provided enough land for the Mission House, more area for the cemetery, and a new parsonage. This area is located four miles southeast of Georgetown near the intersection of County Roads 110 and 111.

In 1852 Calvin Bell settled in the area and it later became known as the Bell Community. It was primarily made up of Swedish families. In 1892 the "Mission House" was built, and in 1908 the parsonage was built. Today the cemetery covers three acres. In 1965, the two acres where the church building and parsonage were located sold to John Rosenblad, which he resold a few months later.

The first burial was of Pearl Lawson in 1889, three years prior to the land possession of the Free Swedish Evangelical Church. She was the infant daughter of Johannes Julius Lawson, a charter member of the church. The reasons as to why Mr. Gustafson allowed Mr. Lawson to bury his four-month-old child on this hillside has been lost to history. However, ongoing research should undercover the connection between the two Swedish gentlemen.

Reverends Who Served

In the history of every denomination there are people who work at the very core of its foundation. This is especially true in the beginning. The life and work of certain individuals have woven themselves into the very fabric of various religion. No matter how old the denomination might be, or how widely it might have deviated from its earliest origin, these people will always keep their places in recorded events and hold a great influence among believers.

The Georgetown Evangelical Free Church is no exception to this. The pioneer leaders were, in their own way and day, great men. When one realizes the difficulties under which they labored, one must appreciate their integrity and the influence these Godly men had upon the community that they ministered to. Our pioneer messengers not only had lofty ideals, but were very independent. Because of their independence, they were known as "Lone Warriors of the Lord."

Churches organized in those days were also independent, which became a proud trait, and many of them still exist today. Some churches, however, could hardly be called organized congregations, as no records were kept. No constitutions were adopted. And no prescribed methods of work were followed. Their great ambition was to stay away from all organized denominations, as they were afraid to be connected with any specific religion. Fortunately, the founding members of the Brushy Evangelical Free Church kept records. Within these records it is noted that four of the early pioneer preachers who founded the Free Church movement across America ministered to the Swedish immigrants in Texas. They were: Edward Thorell, Nels Saabye, C.O. Sahlstrom, and Alex Klint.

Pioneer Messengers

The following messages and/or character descriptions of the former pastors were taken from *The Golden Jubilee: Reminiscences of Our Work Under God,* Swedish Evangelical Free Church of the U.S.A. 1884-1934, and the *Golden Jubilee Reminiscence 1891-1941,* Brushy Evangelical Free Church 1891-1841. However, gone but not forgotten were several pastors who departed from this life to be with the Lord before a formal greeting or acknowledgement about their ministry at the Georgetown Free Church could be recorded. Fortunately, through a relative, a statement was provided on their behalf for this book.

Edward Thorell, known as the mountaineer general, ministered in 1889.

"Leaf after leaf drops off, flower after flower, Some in the chill, some in the warmer hour; Alive they flourished, and alive they fall. And earth who nourished them receives them all. Should all her wiser sons be less content to sink into her lap when life is spent?"—Lander

But it did seem strange that our brother should go so soon. Thorell was not an old man, and his life did not seem spent. But his work was over and he passed on. Although Preacher Thorell was a circuit-rider in Texas during the late 1800s, he great life-work was centered in the Rockies. He was not the founder of the church in Denver, Colorado, but he brought that work to a place of singular success. Through his masterful leadership that church became the leading church among the Scandinavian-speaking people of Denver. Thorell could not confine his interest and driving energy to one place. He was instrumental in opening work in several other cities and towns in Colorado. During the mining boom days, this general of the Lord sent workers into various places and kept them there until work was established. He had faith in God and in himself. In his later years, after having terminated his pastorate in Denver, Thorell was engaged in various fields of activity. It did not seem, however, that he could fully adjust himself to these newer activities. He seemed more or less restless if not entirely dissatisfied. His last field was that of pastor of a little church in Salt Lake City, Utah.

Nels Saabye, known as a crown prince, ministered in 1890.

"And when the battle's over I shall wear a crown, I shall wear a crown, I shall wear a crown. And when the battle's over I shall wear a crown, in the one Jerusalem."

No sketch could be made of this sweet singer in Israel and omit mention of this song. Perhaps he will sing it until he is crowned in glory. Somehow one feels that this song belongs to Brother Saabye. In the early days of the Evangelical Free Church work, Saabye was much in demand. Like most of the pioneers, his gifts were principally the evangelist's. He traveled quite extensively and spent a lot of time in the southwest. A considerable number of the Christian friends in Texas count their spiritual awakening from the late 1800s. Nels was born in Sjien, Norway on June 23, 1851 and came to America in 1882. He attended a Bible Course under Frederick Franson in Chicago and was ordained in Minneapolis for the ministry on October 20, 1894. On May 9, 1895 he married Tina Djones and they were blessed with four children. As an evangelist, he traveled extensively in this country, and as pastor served many churches.

C.O. Sahlstrom, the crying voice in the wilderness, ministered in 1891 and 1892.

Truly as John the Baptist's voice was heard far along the banks of the Jordan and into far-reaching wilderness, so had been Sahlstrom's voice heard over numerous fields. And the method and the message was much of the same—condemnation for sin and exhortation to repentance.

Shortly after the Swedish Free Church in Brushy was erected, Reverend Sahlstrom held services when he was in the area. He traveled also to Decker and Kimbro, and preached to other "Free" congregations between 1891 and 1892. Though successful as pastor of several churches, his greatest success in the evangelistic field where he conducted old-fashioned tent revivals, which seemed to be his life's calling. For this work he had been peculiarly fitted. His name appears early in the Free Church records. He labored long and well, and his reward awaited on the other shore. Sahlstrom was born in Ostergotland, Sweden on Sept. 22, 1852. He came to America in 1879. He married Sara Johnson on August 13, 1885. The couple were blessed with eleven children. His ordination for the ministry took place in Fremont, Iowa in 1881. He served as a traveling evangelist before his service as a fulltime pastor.

Alex Klint, known as the "pioneer poet," ministered in 1897, 1903-1904.

"Shout joyfully to the Lord, all the earth; Break forth and sing for joy and sing praises. Sing praises to the Lord with the lyre; With the lyre and the sound of melody. With trumpets and the sound of the horn. Shout joyfully before the King, the Lord." Psalms 98: 4-6

Brother Klint sung his way into many hearts, which brought cheer and comfort to the troubled soul. He served the Swedish Free Church as pastor a short time in 1897 and again between 1903 to 1904. He also served other Free Churches before he spent the sunset of his life in picturesque Colorado Springs at the foot of the mighty snow-capped Rockies. He was among the first of the Free Church workers with his name appearing early in the records, as it does in the Swedish Free Church in Brushy. He was poetically gifted and therefore loved song and music. He possessed a wonderfully rich and clear voice which he used to the glory of God throughout his entire life. Many were blessed through Brother Klint's singing. Perhaps that was his greatest gift, although he was also a gifted speaker—teaching as true to the Word of God as his voice rang true to harmony. He was the pastor to a number of churches in Minnesota, Nebraska, and Texas. For a number of years Klint traveled as field secretary, and many will long remember these visits and the blessings received.

Gustaf F. Johnson, known as our Brushy Evangelist, ministered the summer of 1896.

"For thus the Lord has commanded us, 'I have placed you as a light for the Gentiles, that you should bring salvation to the end of the earth'." Acts 13:47

"Dear Friends,

Is it really true that half century lies between us and that glorious spiritual springtime, when this church made its modest debut? How our hearts respond with quickened beats to the resurrection of tender memories of long ago! Those days were days of awakening, of revival, of shouting joy and unquenchable fervor. Perfection dwelt not with us, for Youth blunders because of inexperience, but the band of love held us close to God and to one another. The pulpit was not characterized by erudition or profundity, but the intensity of the heart was there.

The lowly cottage that was Father's and Mother's home, had housed many a stirring meeting of kindred souls long ere we ever had thought of church organization or church building. But the few can do exploits when God is their strength; hence we commemorate today the tenacious conviction and unfailing devotion of those joyful days of long ago. The strong leaders of that day have left us one by one, until few are left. If the Grace of God guides the children into the straight paths of the Fathers, a victorious future if this church is assured.

This church was founded on Faith in Jesus Christ, Loyalty to the Word of God, Regeneration through the Holy Spirit, and Separation from the world, with an attitude of looking for the Lord's return. May it continue in that highway of salvation until it is taken home.

Sincerely," Gustaf F. Johnson

Reverend Johnson was born in Nassjo, Sweden on December 27, 1873, and immigrated to Brushy, Texas with his family in 1883. Converted young, he began at age sixteen to witness to the surrounding Swedish-American community with startling results. After a period of service with the Franson Mission in Japan, Johnson returned to the states and became a pastor and evangelist.

August Modig: "Preach the word; be constant in season, out of season; reprove, rebuke, exhort with all long suffering and doctrine." II Timothy 4: 2

Reverend Modig was born in Sweden and immigrated to America in 1894 at the age of nineteen. As a young man, he served the church in 1899. The Free Church found him to be a successful pastor and for many years. He was entrusted with the responsible position of Finance Secretary of the Free Church of America. In 1910 he lived in the Laird Township, Phelps County, Nebraska and was pastor at the Christian's Orphans Home. In 1930 he moved to Minneapolis, Minnesota. and became a Lutheran clergyman.

William N. Nelson: "A wonderful Savior is Jesus my Lord, A wonderful Savior to me, He hideth my soul in the cleft of the rock, Where rivers of pleasure I see."

"Dear Friends,

Heartiest congratulations on this your 50th Anniversary. How we should have enjoyed to have been with you on this occasion, but that is not possible. We shall never forget the time we spent with you forty years ago. We were all somewhat younger then, those who were born, but we are glad to still be alive. It was a thrilling experience to have the opportunity if visiting the Brushy Church again after a period of thirty-seven years. This was in 1938. What a joy to meet the old friends and many of their children, but so many were missing. Some had gone to their eternal rest, others had moved to other places, and a number had lost interest in going to church.

We earnestly hope and pray for God's richest blessing upon the church for future years. We hope many of the younger generations will take a stand for the Lord and fill in the gaps as they occur. With much love we are, Fraternally yours," W.N. Nelson and family

Carl G. Athell: "Great is the Lord, and greatly to be praised in the city of our God, in the mountain of his holiness." Psalm 48:1

Reverend Athell was born in Ljungby, Kalmar Lan, Sweden on May 10, 1878, and came to America October 2, 1900. In preparation for the ministry he attended Augustans College, Rock Island, Illinois; the Free Church School in Chicago; and took a two year course at the Y.M.C.A., in Seattle, Washington. He was ordained for the ministry in New Windsor, Illinois in 1901. He served the Swedish Free Church of Brushy between the fall of 1905 to the spring of 1908. After serving as pastor to a number of churches he traveled as a evangelist for three years, and then returned to Sweden where he ministered as an evangelist.

Carl J. E. Nelson: "But, beloved, we are persuaded better things of you, and things that accompany salvation, though we thus speak. For God is not unrighteous to forget your work and labor of love, which ye have shown toward His name in that ye have ministered to the saints, and do minister." Hebrews 6:9-10, 19

"Greetings in the Name of our Lord and Savior, Jesus Christ.

Behold what manner of love the Father hath bestowed upon us, that we should be called the sons of God; therefore the world know us not, because it knew Him not. Beloved, now are we the sons of God, and it doth not yet appear what we shall be; but we know that, when He shall appear, we shall be like Him; for we shall see Him as He is.

We are more than thirty years closer to the goal and our heavenly home than we were when we first met and began our ministry of the Word to you. The two years that we spent at Brushy and labored though very inefficient, due to ill health, will never be forgotten. We have many blessed memories from these two years and know that some are still following the Lord that during our ministry accepted Christ as their Savior. There are very few of the old saints left at Brushy that were active in the work during our ministry, but we are glad that so many of a later generation are carrying on the work of the forefathers and following in their footsteps. Your labors in the Lord is not in vain and He will reward you in due time.

We often talk about days gone by and your kindness in every way during our affliction. The sympathy and financial aid before we left your midst is remembered by us and recorded in heaven, and we can say as the apostle Paul and change Thessalonica to Colorado. 'For even in Colorado ye sent once and again unto my (our) necessity' (Philippines 4:16). We would like to say all the good things about you that we can think of and what we do not remember we want to add to it. We would like to mention you all by name and every kind deed, but space will not permit. We want to thank you so much for the invitation to be present at your Golden Jubilee. In reply to this invitation we want to answer with the apostle Paul: 'Only let your conversation be as it becometh the gospel of Christ: that whether I (we) come and see you, or else be absent, I (we) may hear of your affairs, that ye stand fast in one spirit, with one mind striving together for the faith of the gospel' (Philippines 1:27). Yours in Him," Carl J. E. Nelson and family.

Reverend Nelson served the Brushy church between the fall of 1908 to spring of 1910.

H.A. Gustin: May it please the Lord to say to you as to the church in Thyatira: "I know thy works, and the last to be more than the first."

"Christian Greetings!

The celebration of your Golden Jubilee turns my thoughts to bygone days—almost thirty years ago when Mrs. Gustin and I were in your midst. Then were we young and inexperienced, but we loved the Lord and were interested in His cause.

The church membership was then, as now, largely made of friends who were in their prime of life, and not a few were children in our Sunday school. Now you have taken up the fallen mantles of your elders who have gone on to their reward and you are faithfully continuing the work that they had so well begun. At this time of 'reminiscing' we bless you, their children. I always look back to the four years I had the privilege of being your pastor as among the happiest of my life. I have many cherished memories from the days. Memories which will never be forgotten. Some of them are associated with the many and well-attended cottage meetings and at Berry's Creek and at Jonah.

I regarded brother C.O. Youngbloom as an ideal chairman and C. H. Gustafson as a man who held a rather unique place in the church as well as in the community at large. But there were many others whom I regarded highly and counted as my true friends. The Brushy Church has always stood on the firm foundation of God's holy Word, which has been faithfully taught to the children in Sunday school and in no uncertain tones been proclaimed from the pulpit. The various brothers who served you as pastor for a longer or shorter period were happy to know that the Brushy Church held an influential place in the life of the community and that the work there carried on was not in vain. Accept our heartiest congratulations on your having reached the fiftieth milestone . . . half a century of ministry with and for the Lord—as a church. May this be indeed a happy Golden Jubilee celebration." H.A. Gustin

Reverend Gustin was born on August 22, 1884. He attended the Bible Institute of the Swedish Evangelical Free Church in preparation for the ministry. He served as pastor to the Decker Free Church, and Brushy Free Church (January 1911-May 1915). After leaving Texas, he became superintendent of the Christian Orphans' Home of Holdrege, Nebraska. On January 25, 1911 he married Ruby D. Anderson and the couple had two children.

E.H. Lindquist: Grace and Peace of God in Jesus Christ! "Lord, Thou hast been our dwelling place in all generations." Psalm 90:1

"Dearest Friends,

We think back with much pleasure on the years 1915-1920, spent in Brushy Free Church. The kindness shown us and the friendship never to be forgotten. We remember the blessings of God in the meetings. We think of the large tent meetings. We think of the souls that sought the Lord for salvation. The years have rolled by. It is now twenty-one years since we left. Those who were boys and girls then are now nearing middle age. Those who were young people then are now at the head of the work and are carrying the main load: also supplying the leadership of the Church.

Many of those who then were leaders are now resting beneath the sod in the shadow of the more recently-built edifice.

But God's cause goes marching on. We congratulate the Brushy Free Church in fulfilling fifty years of service for the Lord that it has been a burning and shining light in the community. That no one has needed to go to destruction and perdition for want of knowing of the Gospel in that region. The church has been a city on the hill. A place to which the weary souls have been refreshed. The sin-sick have found peace with God there. The children have found instruction in the Word of God there. They have received knowledge of their need of the Savior and they have had opportunity to find that Savior there.

'Just a few more days, to be filled with grace, and to tell the old, old story. Then when twilight falls and the Savior calls we'll go to be with Him in glory.' Till then, may the Brushy Free Church, with its pastor, its corps of workers, its membership of veterans, prime age men and women, its youth and the children, may all be faithful till that day.

May the Gospel light always shine forth clearly from the Evangelical Free Church at Brushy, Texas. Your old friends and co-workers," Esther and E. H. Lindquist.

Reverend Lindquist was born on May 18, 1884 in Watertown, Minnesota. He received his education for the ministry at the Free Church Bible Institute in Chicago, and was ordained on May 23, 1903 at Watertown. He was the pastor of several churches in Nebraska, California, Texas, and Washington. As an evangelist, he served Nebraska and California societies, and was the Superintendent of the Western District Society. On June 14, 1906 he married Esther Nyberg and they had seven children. He served the Brushy church between 1915 to 1920.

John Udd: "Grace to you and peace from God our Father and the Lord Jesus Christ. I thank my God always concerning you, for the grace of God which was given you in Christ Jesus, that in everything you were enriched in Him, in all speech and all knowledge, even as the testimony concerning Christ was confirmed in you, so that you are not lacking in any gift, awaiting eagerly the revelation of our Lord Jesus Christ." I Corinthians 1:3-7

"Christian Greetings Dear Friends,

It has been eighteen years sense we left Brushy. Time has passed unusually quick. We had much gladness and fond memories from the short time we were among you at the Brushy church. We are grateful for your kindness. We thank God always for you and your work in the church. We hope that you have a blessed 50th Jubilee." John Udd

Reverend John Udd was born in Wasa, Finland on September 4,1866 and came to America in 1888. In preparation for the ministry he pursued studies for three years at the Chicago Theological Seminary, and ordained in 1896. As pastor he served the Swedish Congregational Church of Worcester, Massachusetts, and the Free Churches at Ludington, Michigan; Cambridge, Massachusetts; Denver, Colorado; Holdrege, Nebraska; Kimbro, Manor, and Brushy, Texas; and Greeley, Colorado. On June 4, 1906, he married to Amalia Anderson and they had four children. He was pastor of the Brushy church from 1920 to 1922.

Alfred Stone: "Remember His marvelous works that He hath done." Psalm 105:5

"Dear Members and Friends of the Evangelical Free Church or Brushy, Texas.

A greeting to you, our friends, at this particular time is a great pleasure for me to comply with. A few years have now passed by since we had the great pleasure to serve you. During these years God has been our Strength and All. You will be happy to know that we have refreshing from above. I deeply appreciate, for Christ's sake and the great work for our Lord, your sincere prayer for us in the work we are privileged to continue.

In these trying, confusing, perplexing days of world distress, I am so glad we have the Word of God to lead us and instruct us in the right way. Yes, it is our 'blessed hope.' I am very happy that you now have the opportunity to look back on fifty years of many problems that God alone has been able to help you through and that you are now privileged to celebrate the Fiftieth Anniversary of the founding of your church to the honor and glory of His name alone.

We live in a time which has its great problems of how to get the unsaved into our services but you have a place to invite them—'the open door of the House of God.' Your work, after all, has just begun. As it is said concerning the church at Philadelphia, so with you: 'I know Thy works, behold I have set before thee an open door and no man can shut it.' Yours in everlasting bonds and increasing hope for the coming of our Lord." Alfred Stone.

Reverend Stone was born in Orebro Lan, Narke, Sweden on March 24, 1874, and came to America in 1897. In preparation for the ministry he attended the North Park College and the Swedish Bible Institute of Chicago, Illinois. On March 19, 1905 he was ordained to the ministry and in 1906 he went to Japan as a missionary. Due to illness he returned to America and has served numerous churches throughout Texas, Washington, Oregon, Nebraska, Colorado, and Minnesota, etc. He married Julia Thompson on August 23, 1911 and they had two children. He served the Brushy church between December 1922 to 1925.

Carl A. Malme: "Upon this Rock shall I build my Church." Matthew 16:18

"Beloved in The Lord,

As it has pleased God to bestow upon you, as a Church, the opportunity to celebrate the Golden Jubilee, I take pleasure in sending you my sincere congratulation, rejoicing with you, in this wonderful Grace of God, and the honor that has come to you as a group of God's children.

With great joy I look back upon the years God permitted me to labor among you as your pastor. Our preaching was not with worldly wisdom but, I trust, in the power of God, that your faith should not be by worldly wisdom, but by the Power of God. Christ is the Rock on which His church, and people are built and the material of which Christ's church is built are chosen out of the world, and He employees many hands in carrying out the building. He himself is the Master-builder. Our Free Church Pioneer Preachers, had the honor of laying the first stones, by many converts, in the Brushy Free Church, they did not build upon themselves, but upon 'this Rock.' Some of you are still active in the work will remember the Godly men and women who labored in the church at Brushy from its early beginning. The pioneers have gone to be with the lord, to receive their reward, and to you, the present members of the church are given the glorious opportunity to continue the work. It is your blessed privilege to live the life of complete surrender. You can make your church a spirit-filled and a surrendered church. All the power of God is within our reach if we only obey Him. Yours in Christ," Carl A. Malme.

Reverend Malme was born on March 24, 1883 at Kristiansand, Norway, and came to America in 1903. He attended the Salvation Army Training College, the Free Church Bible Institute, and also took a correspondence course from the Augsburg Seminary. His ordination for the ministry took place at Stillman Valley, Illinois, on August 29, 1908. He married Hattie Anderson on December 28, 1907, and they had three children. He was pastor of the Brushy church between the spring of 1925 to June 1930.

Eric W. Frohman: "Thanks be unto God for His unspeakable gift." 2 Corinthians. 9:15

"Dearest Friends,

It is with much pleasure that I send you a greeting for the Golden Jubilee. we know that at this particular time you will recall things that are deeply engraved upon your hearts. As you remember these outstanding impressions you will also be reminded of God's faithfulness. But, He who has been with you through both sunshine and shadows changes not, will guide you to new victories. Our ministry in Brushy will always be remembered, and as the fragrance of those years invigorate us we cannot help, but, out of the depths of our hearts thank God for your faithful work in the church. May the coming years be just a fruitful, and more so, in that you continue to work for the Master. The work that the pioneers laid down has accomplished great things for God, and may this generation be inspired and strengthened by the Holy Ghost to go on even to greater success.

We join with you in singing, 'Praise God from whom all Blessings Flow,' and earnestly pray God's continued Grace upon each one of you. Yours in the Master's service," E.W. Frohman.

Reverend Frohman was born in Sweden. In preparation for the ministry he pursued studies and graduated at the Free Church Bible Institute of Chicago, Illinois. He served as pastor in California, Nebraska, and Texas. In March 1928 he married Edith Rodman and they had two children. He was pastor of the Brushy church between spring 1931 to August 1934.

N.J. Christensen: "They that wait on the Lord shall renew their strength: they shall mount up with eagle wings; they shall run and not be weary; they shall walk and not faint." Isaiah 40:31

"Dearest Friends,

The eagle is known as the king of birds, it is not content to dwell in low regions but soars into the heavens. Only eagles are born with eagle wings. The children of God are likened unto the eagle. They cannot feel at home in the low altitudes but long for the higher regions. Through a new birth they become recipients of a power that enables them to 'mount up with eagle wings.'

Fifty years ago a small group of believers waited upon the Lord. As a result of this waiting the Brushy Church was born. For half a century it has stood as a lighthouse on a hill. Souls have found Christ, believers have been blessed, and children have been instructed in the Word of God. The pastors who have served this church during these years, have been men who have stressed the necessity of a new birth in order to receive power from on high.

As one of your former pastors, who has had fellowship with you for more than five years. I send warmest congratulations. The church after these fifty years, is much stronger numerically than it was when it started half a century ago. Unless the eagle wings are lacking to lift if toward new heights, it is bound to have a glorious future because its members believe in waiting upon the God, hence their strength is renewed. Without the relationship with God the Brushy Church will like many others, struggle, flutter and fall into oblivion. Then this little book will become an obituary of another church which failed to appropriate God's power and program. This, God forbid. May God's blessing rest upon the Brushy Church for many years to come. Sincerely," N. J. Christensen

Reverend Christensen was born on January 6, 1897. He graduated from the Moody Bible Institute and the Free Church Bible Institute, both of Chicago, Illinois. For six years he served as missionary in the Free Church Mission Field in North China. In 1921 he married Mella Hedberg and they had two children. He served the Brushy church between September 1934 to January 1940.

Morris Rosene: "Thou wilt keep him in perfect peace, whose mind is stayed on Thee: because he trusteth in Thee." Isa. 26:3.

Reverend Rosen was pastor of the Brushy Church during its Golden Jubilee, therefore did not submit a greeting. He was born at Stromsburg, Nebraska on November 16, 1895. He graduated from the Free Church Bible Institute and the Moody Bible Institute both of Chicago, Illinois. On

September 3, 1924 he entered into holy matrimony and the couple had one child. He served the Brushy church between August 1940 to August 1951.

Arthur Anderson: "For Jehovah God is our Light and our Protector. He gives us grace and glory. No good thing will He withhold from those who walk along His paths." Psalm 84:11

Reverend Anderson was born on April 24, 1903., in Princeton, Minnesota. He graduated from the Bible Institute of the Minnehaha Academy, Minneapolis, Minnesota and attended Bethel Seminary of St. Paul where he earned a Th.B. degree in 1931, and from Macalester College in 1933 with an A.B. degree. During his ministry he served as pastor in Marathon and Center Grove, Iowa; Loomis, Nebraska; Watertown, Minnesota; and Georgetown, Texas (August 1951 to May 1956). During his last twelve years of ministry, he was the Administrator of the Evangelical Free Church Home for the Aged in Boone, Iowa. He married to Violet Johnson on June 27, 1933. The couple had three daughters: Enid, Rosalie and Carmen.

Bertil Thorne: "When we all get to heaven, What a day of rejoicing that will be! When we all see Jesus, We'll sing and shout the victory."

Reverend Thorne was born in Melvin, Texas in 1910. He attended the Evangelical Free Church (organized in 1910) in Melvin with his family until completion of High School. He graduated from Trinity Bible College and Seminary in Chicago, Illinois in 1939. Pastor Thorne served, with his wife Miriam Johnson Thorne, in the following churches: Pepin Hill and Ella, Wisconsin; Cairo, Nebraska; Meriden, Iowa; Tacoma, Washington; Princeton, Minnesota; Georgetown and Elgin, Texas. The Thorne family included two daughters, Karen and Sylvia. Pastor and Mrs. Thorne retired in Georgetown after thirty-three years in the ministry. He was honored with the title of Pastor Emeritus in 1988 at the Georgetown Evangelical Free Church. They were loved and supported by many friends over those years. God is Good. He served the Brushy church between August 1956 to January 1965.

E.L. Pearson: "Only trust Him, only trust Him, Only trust Him now; He will save you, He will save you, He will save you, He will save you now."

Reverend Pearson was born in Varmland, Sweden on April 14, 1888, and immigrated to America in 1906. He studied at Augustana College in Rock Island, Illinois, and was ordained to the ministry in March 1918. As a pastor he served churches in Iowa, Nebraska, Minnesota, and Texas. He married Ruth Strombeck of Moline, Illinois on December 10, 1910. They had two children. He served as interim pastor of the Georgetown church between February 1965 to August 1965.

Walter Osborne: "Remember the days of old, consider the years of many generations; ask thy father, and he will shew thee; thy children, and they will tell thee." Deut. 32:7

Reverend Osborne was born in Chicago, Illinois on August 23, 1937. He received his pastoral education at Trinity Seminary. After Osborne retired from the ministry, he worked at Moody Bible Institute as historian and researcher for more than thirty years. He married Dorothy Eisenhut on December 21, 1957. The couple had six children. He was pastor of the Georgetown church between September 1965 to August 1967.

Richard Mittanck: "And there is salvation in no one else; for there is no other name under heaven that has been given among men, by which we must be saved." Acts 4:12

"Greetings, and congratulations on your 120th Anniversary.

I arrived at the Georgetown Evangelical Free Church in the fall of 1967, fresh out of Trinity Seminary, as it was called in those days. While there was much unrest in our Nation at that time, things in Georgetown were rather peaceful, and the congregation warmly took me and my family into their fellowship.

About the only difficulty I had was in placing names with faces: Nord and Youngbloom were relatively easy, but getting the slight difference in Ekdahl and Ekvall was more if a challenge. But, what took the longest was the Johnsons and Andersons—there were so many of them! And if my memory serves me, there was a brother and sister named Anderson, who each married another brother and sister named Anderson! Anyway, the memories are good ones, and everyone was so patient to a young seminarian and his sometimes impatient ways. I trust you will continue to love and encourage one another until He returns.

With Love in Christ," Richard Mittanck

Reverend Mittanck was pastor to the Georgetown church between September 1965 to December 1972.

Larry Larson: "Precious memories, how they linger. How they ever flood my soul. In the stillness of the midnight. Sacred scenes of love unfold."

"I remember my ministry at Georgetown Evangelical Free Church with fondness. We had just come from a church in Minnesota where our lives were moving at ninety miles an hour. How wonderful to have time to slow down and enjoy the fellowship of a precious congregation. We treasure the memories of each one and appreciate each one whose life enriched ours. The faithfulness of your congregation and the dedication of service were a tremendous encouragement to me. It was during this time that Twin Oaks Ranch was still in its infancy and you threw your support behind it. It was a united purpose toward which we put our faith, our money and our efforts. It was at this camp that we had a wonderful church picnic and baptismal service. It was with Twin Oaks Ranch that I had the opportunity to be the Chairman of the board. I was acquainted with camping programs in Minnesota and they thought it might be helpful. I also was both Camp Director and speaker at Twin Oaks one summer at the same camp. That was not my decision, but the experience of wearing two different hats at the same time is something to remember. One of the hats would always be falling off. But God is good—all the time.

God bless you dear people who gave so much. We haven't forgotten you!" Larry Larson

Reverend Larson served the Georgetown church between February 1973 to May 1975.

Raymond Wegner: "Take my life, and let it be Consecrated, Lord to Thee; Take my hands, and let them move At the impulse of Thy love, At the impulse of Thy love."

"I came to Georgetown after graduating from Trinity Evangelical Divinity School, Deerfield, Illinois. I was excited to candidate in Georgetown, for I'm a Southerner from eastern Kentucky, and not a cold-weather person. On my candidacy trip, I came with Joyce, my wife, and our son, Mark, who was just a couple of months old. Hubert and Gretelle Ekvall were our very gracious hosts.

My first view of Georgetown was coming up Church Street with its beautiful trees and homes. I liked it. I was excited to receive the call to come pastor, and this involved driving into the state from the north. When we came to the border of Texas, I told Joyce and our two girls, Anne and Becky, that we were almost home. Was I wrong! Another four to five hour trip was ahead of us.

Coming to Texas was a big adjustment. The parsonage was the first house we lived in as a family (before we'd lived in an apartment). Texas itself was a culture shock—the attitude of Texans, long hot dry summers, and how large the state was.

The pastorate was very enjoyable. I enjoyed the preaching and teaching, visiting, and in short loving people. Office duties were not my forte, and I had wonderful help in that department. During my pastorate, we started monthly pot lucks; I had a men's Bible study; made contacts with some Southwestern students; and encouraged the formation of a Free Church in Round Rock." Ray Wegner.

Reverend Wegner served the Georgetown church between July 1975 to June 1982.

Daryl Walling: "Sitting at the feet of Jesus, O what words I hear Him say! Happy place! So near, so precious! May it find me there each day! Sitting at the feet of Jesus, I would look upon the past; For His love has been so gracious, It has won my heart at last."

Reverend Walling sends his love and congratulations to the church on its 120th Anniversary celebration. He and his family loved serving the church and the congregations needs. He served the Georgetown church between January 1983 to July 1988.

Gordon T. Bakan: "O worship the King all glorious above, And gratefully sing, His wonderful love; Our Shield and Defender, the Ancient of days, Pavilioned in splendor, and girded with praise."

"My wife Janis and I came to Georgetown from South Dakota where we had served an Evangelical Free Church. Coming to Texas was a cultural change for both of us, as I had grown up in California and Janis had grown up in North Dakota. However, we enjoyed our time in Texas and are thankful for the ministry we had in the church.

We lost a lot of members during our time there to death or nursing homes. That was difficult for us because we had become close to those individuals. The highlights of our ministry, other than building relationships with the congregation, were the outreach program 'The Phone's For You' and the church's 100th Anniversary celebration, both of which took place in 1991.

All ministries have their challenges and our ministry in the Georgetown church was no exception, but I would not trade it for anything. I am thankful to the Lord that we were able to serve the church for over six years, and am thankful for all that God did in the lives of the people there through our ministry." Gordon Bakan.

Reverend Bakan served the Georgetown church between October 1988 to January 1995.

Tommy Rosenblad: "O what a wonderful Savior is He, Jesus who suffered on Calvary's tree: Finding me, loving me. Saving and keeping me, Jesus, my Savior and Friend."

"The Georgetown Evangelical Free Church was for me a place of blessed beginnings. The church provided me opportunities to preach while in high school and college. The congregation was always so encouraging. In December of 1994 when they asked if I would be interested in serving as the Interim Pastor, especially since I was just about to turn twenty, I was surprised. And a few months later, they called me to serve as their full time pastor. I am so thankful for those people who gave such a young and inexperienced person as I was an opportunity to serve.

Needless to say that experience involved a lot of mistakes that the members were willing to overlook and continued to help me find my way as a minister. It was a time I look back on with such gratitude. God used that experience to confirm my life's call of being a pastor." Tommy Rosenblad

Reverend Rosenblad served the Georgetown church between December 1994 to Spring 1998.

Louis A. Herman: "O what a wonder that Jesus found me, Out in the darkness, no light could I see; O what a wonder, He put His great arm under, And wonder of wonder, He saved even me!"

"The Georgetown Evangelical Free Church was a time of blessing for my wife, and I. We served for only a few months in 1998, but I know it was God's will, and many things were accomplished during this time.

We were new to Texas, and the church really made us feel welcome. Pastor Tommy Rosenblad encouraged us to serve the church. The first time

I met Pastor David Gauthier he had just graduated from the Moody Bible Institute. He was very honest, and told me that he felt called to pastor the church. Shortly after this, Pastor Scott Willis in Chicago wanted us to serve the Lord with him. He had gotten saved in our church when we were in Illinois, and then later he and his wife lost six children in a van accident. We felt called to minister to them in this time of healing. Also, the City College of Chicago offered me a position as Vice Chancellor of Technology.

Everett and Frieda Ryden were special friends, and they later visited us in Chicago on their way to Sweden. Charlie and Virginia Johnson would come over and we would go cruising in one of their old antique cars. Charlie had me to study a big blue book on the Swedish history of Texas, and he also sang a Swedish song as a special. Virginia made the best ice tea ever. Margie Youngbloom was a saint used to glorify God. I visited Wesley Nord at his farm, and seeing cotton for the first time. He was faithful in giving out the church bulletins each Sunday. Hubert and Gretell were also very helpful and hospitable to us. In the church, so many showed us the love of Christ, and we thank God for each dear soul. I am so thankful the Lord allowed me to teach and preach the Word, and pastor the Georgetown Evangelical Free Church." Lou Herman

The Present Pastor

David Gauthier: "Therefore, since we have this ministry, as we received mercy, we do not lose heart, but we have renounced the things hidden because of shame, not walking in craftiness or adulterating the word of God, but by the manifestation of truth, commending ourselves to every man's conscience in the sight of God." 2 Cor. 4:1-2

"I grew up in Georgetown—a stone's throw from the church, in fact. But I was not raised in a Christian home, so I never gave a second thought about the Free Church at the corner of University Ave. and Hutto Rd, as I rode by it on my bike countless times. But the Lord had other plans.

After I became a Christian, I attended Moody Bible Institute, in Chicago, Ill. and graduated in May of 1998 with a degree in Pastoral Studies. I began to look for a place to serve in ministry. Unlike my fellow classmates at Moody, who were eager to serve anywhere in the world that God was leading them, I sensed the conviction that the Lord wanted for me to 'go home'—that meant Georgetown. That first Sunday upon returning to Georgetown, Kristi and I attended the Georgetown Evangelical Free Church. At the time, there were only about a dozen faithful, but mostly elderly, people in attendance. But we felt so loved and accepted that we decided to joined the church.

The church had just extended a call to their interim pastor, Lou Herman, to be their full-time minister. In all honesty, I recall initially feeling just a touch of disappointment at first, knowing that I had sent a resume to GEFC, but was never asked about it.

One Sunday in late August, without expectation, Pastor Lou Herman read a letter of resignation to the church, following his sermon. And then, in a stunning statement, Pastor Lou suddenly looked at me and boldly said, 'Besides, I just don't see the sense in my filling the pulpit when you've got a young guy *right here* that you could ask to be your pastor!'

I think my heart stopped. My breathing did, anyway. My brother and his wife happened to be in attendance that morning, for which I am thankful. We were all floored by the comment. Truly, I was vexed by it all—I couldn't believe he said that, especially without any warning. I felt honored and humbled, yet simultaneously quite concerned that perhaps others in the church were thinking that I had pushed Pastor Lou out!

In the weeks that followed, I met with the church board, chaired by Tillman Johnson. I recall the awkward dance of negotiation that transpired. I had assumed that, despite Pastor Lou's hearty recommendation, perhaps they may not *want* me to be their pastor. And yet I learned from Tillman that the board was wondering if *I* would want to be their pastor!

On September 20, 1998, I preached my first sermon 'The God We Rely Upon,' which seemed very fitting—at least in my case.

Since those earliest days, the church has grown in various ways, seeing people of all ages weave in and out of its history. We have been through thick and thin, but one thing that has *never* changed in all my time here is the loving acceptance of this church family." David Gauthier

EARLY SWEDISH IMMIGRATION

Stephen F. Austin was the Father of Texas,
but Swante M. Swenson was the Father of Swedish Immigration to Texas.

Stephen F. Austin legally claimed and ultimately colonized Brazoria County in southeast Texas between 1823 to 1825 by emigrating 300 families from the United States; yet, not one of those families were Swedish. On the other hand, through the efforts of Swante M. Swenson, twenty-five Swedish immigrants arrived in 1848 from Barkeryd, Smaland, Sweden, which led to the arrival of around 125 additional immigrants to Williamson and Travis counties before the outbreak of the Civil War in 1861.

Swante Swenson, the first Swedish immigrant to settle on Texas soil, arrived in 1838. Two years prior, this journey to Texas came to an abrupt halt when the ship that he was aboard from Sweden burned upon its arrival in New York harbor. Thus he came ashore with only the clothes on his back. For a brief time he stayed in the city where he worked as a store clerk and learned English. He eventually went to Baltimore, Maryland and he worked as a railroad bookkeeper before he made his way to Brazoria County, Texas. There he worked for John Adriance, who operated a large mercantile business. Swenson peddled goods from an ambulance type carriage bearing the sign "Columbus Supply House." While making his rounds, he befriended Dr. George Long, a plantation owner near Richmond in Fort Bend County. Long was in poor health and hired Swenson to become his overseer. After Long's death in 1842, his widow returned to Tennessee to visit relatives and Swenson supervised the plantation. The following year Swenson purchased a neighboring plantation and, in

December, he married Dr. Long's widow, Jeanette Long. Needless to say, through Swenson's shrewd dealings he became wealthy.

In 1844 Swenson's uncle, Swante Palm, arrived; he was the first Swede to immigrate to America with Texas as his specific destination. Palm helped Swenson with his numerous, and prosperous, business ventures such as real estate investments and finances generated by his cotton plantation in Fort Bend County.

Over the years, Swante Swenson became a friend and admirer of Sam Houston, who urged Swante to recruit Swedish immigrants to settle the sparsely-occupied interior of Texas. Swenson did what Houston suggested. He went to Sweden in 1847 to recruit families from his home parish of Barkeryd in northern Smaland. That first year, his sister accompanied him back to Texas. The next year, however, a group of twenty-five people, related to one another or to Swenson or Swante Palm, either by birth or through marriage, became the first party of Swedes to follow the journey Palm had made four years prior. This was only the beginning as half the citizens of Barkeryd immigrated to Texas between 1848 to 1927.

The group initially joined Swenson in Fort Bend County; however, Swenson sold his cotton plantation and its attendant slaves shortly after their arrival and moved to a large cattle ranch east of Austin, which he named "Govalle" after a Swedish phrase meaning "good grazing."

Govalle became Swenson's home for more than ten years. During this time it also became the first home of new Swedish immigrants who had arrived in their New World. Swenson and Palm arranged their passage to Texas, and they, in turn, worked for their benefactors to pay off the price of the ticket, which took about two years. After the debt was paid off they were free to live and work for themselves. Most of the immigrants purchased land from Swenson, who owned more than 100,000 acres around the Austin area, and farmed cotton.

By the 1860s many Swedish communities around Central Texas had been settled by the Barkeryd immigrants. Williamson County had the most contiguous rural colonies: Brushy Creek, Palm Valley, Hutto, Jonah, Taylor, and Round Rock. On the Blackland Prairie, in northeast Travis County, Swedes began to settle after the Civil War in 1865. They established the colonies of New Sweden, Manor, Kimbro, Manda, and Lund. Almost all of these areas were devoted to cotton production.

Among the twenty-five members of Swenson's family who arrived in 1848 was Anders Palm, his wife Anna, and their six children. Anders died soon after arrival, leaving Anna the first widow among the Swedish immigrants. She and her children moved in 1849 to a farm in Washington County. In 1953 they moved and settled in Williamson County near Round Rock which they named Palm Valley. At first the family lived in a tent, but later built a nice home that was always open to welcome their new kinsmen to the area. Presently, the Palm house has been relocated to Main Street in Round Rock and is home to the Chamber of Commerce, which continues to welcome visitors to the city.

When the Civil War ended, the slave trade was declared illegal. A new era in Texas history began when the shortage of workers became a problem. This condition was the primary factor in the increasing number of Swedish immigration at the end of the 1860s. Plantation owners needed workers and since there was no law that prohibited making contracts and importing foreigners, Swente Swenson, and his uncle Swente Palm, and Swenson's relative Johan, who lived in Sweden, began to run an informal Swedish immigration service often referred to as the "Swedish pipeline."

The first Swedes who made contracts to come from Sweden to work on plantations were known as "Free Sons of the North." They yearned for their own home under their own "soot blackened rooftop." Their time on these plantations was only as long as necessary to pay for their passage and the price of a pair of oxen and a plow. Land was inexpensive and was mostly bought on credit, and so the hard work of cultivation began which transformed the rough prairie into fertile fields.

Between 1865 and 1871, from the small parish of Barkeryd alone, 184 Swedes left for Texas. In 1868 Sweden became the target of a famine. The catastrophic year left little or no food to feed the many citizens, or money to buy food. It was no wonder that an offer to travel three to four months to Texas, and other parts of America, was so agreeable to these people. In the summer of 1867 the *Georgetown Watchman* reported that 75 Swedes arrived in Williamson County on May 31. These immigrants were scattered throughout the community to different homesteads such as those of the Palms, the Nelsons, and to other wealthy Swedes to work off the cost of their passage.

The Palms had a trusted a young Negro man that lived with them in Palm Valley and who also carried the Palm surname, Will Palm. Orphaned at a young age, the boy was educated and trained with children of the Palm home and learned to speak Swedish fluently. Sometimes when emigrants from Sweden were due in the area, William Palm sent the

Negro youth to meet and welcome, and assist them to their destinations, as he communicated with them in their native language. The curiosity of one fair-skinned group of Scandinavians was too much for them when they saw the dark-skinned Negro, and they asked him about it. While still speaking in Swedish, Will jokingly explained that this was a natural result of the hot Texas sun and it simply turned a person's skin dark. The newcomers took him seriously and were very impressed with the strange and marvelous power of the Texas sun.

Although the Swedish community in Texas is larger than in any other southern state, it has never played a dominant role in the state culture or politics. A single newspaper the *Texas-Posten* was published in Austin from 1896 to 1981 to serve the interest of the group. There were two higher education facilities: Trinity Lutheran College of Round Rock, chartered in 1906, and Texas Wesleyan College at Austin, chartered in 1912. Due to insufficient financial support, in 1929 Trinity merged with Texas Lutheran College in Seguin, and the Texas Wesleyan sold its grounds to the University of Texas in 1931.

In honor of the large number of immigrants to Texas from Barkeryd, the people of Barkeryd parish, Smaland were proclaimed honorary citizens of Texas on May 27, 1975 by Governor Dolph Briscoe.

Footnote: According to the Swedish language, the word parish is not capitalized.

BRUSHY COLONY

The Brushy Colony, the heart of the Swedish communities in Williamson County, was located east of Georgetown, north of Palm Valley, bordered Jonah to the north and Hutto to the east.

The name Brushy was not used for this area in the beginning; it was first applied to the area along Brushy Creek, where the first Swedes in Texas settled in the early 1850s. Today the area is called Palm Valley. Brushy became the universal name for the area between Hutto and Round Rock from the Brushy Creek in the south, to Georgetown in the north. Within this area, three different churches developed; the Lutheran, the Methodist (1882), and the Free Church (all of which called their congregations "Brushy"). Many times a stranger who was unfamiliar with the situation would ask, "Where is the real Brushy Community located?" Well, they were all real. But the original Brushy was the first name for Georgetown where a post office was established in 1847 when the area was still part of Milam County. Brushy Creek, established in 1851 was the early name for the community of Round Rock.

In 1906 the Methodists sold their country-church and built a Gothic Revival Sanctuary in Georgetown. The name was changed to St. John's United Methodist Church. The Lutheran Church, established in 1870, took the name Swedish Evangelical Lutheran Brushy Church. Today it is known as Palm Valley Lutheran Church and is located on the original acreage donated by Swante M. Swenson, the first Swedish immigrant of Texas.

The Free Church congregation took the name Brushy Evangelical Free Church as their official name. Even though the church was located in the county, in 1951 the congregation charged the name to the Evangelical Free Church of Georgetown. In 1963 when the church actually moved to the city, the named was changed for a third time to Georgetown Evangelical Free Church.

The Brushy Community was quite an attractive area. From the top of the Free Church Mission House, as far as the eye could see, there were beautiful white-painted Swedish farmhouses in every direction: toward Georgetown to the west, Weir in the north, Taylor to the east, and Round Rock to the south. The Swedes were fairly well off economically. Most of them who settled here immigrated in the early 1880s.

Early Pioneers of the Swedish Free Church

Life of the pioneer was far from easy, and at times far from pleasant. The pioneer battled with the powers of an unexplored earth that rebuked mankind's efforts to tame its resources. The earth ignored the pioneers' struggles and offered no comfort beyond the presence of the earth itself.

But the earth was always there, with its woods and hills and rocks, and with its endless prairies. The prairies were not the easiest lands to subdue. To work all day in the blazing Texas sun with no relief from the insufferable glare, was not easy. The only let-up after sundown was the grayness of nightfall.

Pioneer women must have found it particularly hard, especially those who emigrated from cooler Scandinavian Peninsula. Many of them, at one time or another, had come from good homes and well organized settlements or parishes, while others had come from larger cities. All of them, however, came into this vast loneliness and terrifying silence. At times they must have been filled with nameless fear, and through that fear they grew weary.

But fear created character, in both men and women. It either built stamina or it destroyed them. For the most part, fear made them stronger. The strength that shone in their eyes seemed to be ignited by sunrays and the vastness of outdoors. The pioneers found their happiness not in the comforts and frills of life, but in their faith. They were dominated by a philosophy in which success depended not upon their state of mind, but upon disciplined thinking, faith, and hard work. Through their rugged determination they learned by and through various experiences that the first knockdown is not always a knockout, and there was always a chance until the last count and final sound of the bell to indicate the fight was over.

This can also be said about Christian pioneers and their work. Theirs too was a time of great conquest. The means and methods they used to meet the demands of the hour were done undoubtedly though prayer and faith. To them the trials and tribulations were preeminent and as time went on new attitudes unfolded. The feelings of discernment started to rise like a misty fog and slowly disappeared, leaving God's children to unite with Christian love that formed the brotherhood and sisterhood of believers within the Brushy Evangelical Free Church.

Carl Edward Anderson family

Carl Edward Anderson was born in Axberg parish, Narke, Sweden in 1865, and moved to Oggestorp, Smaland, Sweden as a young boy. His parents, Sven and Britta Anderson, were farmers. In 1884, Carl immigrated to Round Rock, Texas where he lived in the home of Gustaf Johnson and worked the land. After Carl became a tenant farmer, he and his family lived near Georgetown for about twelve years, and then purchased a farm west of Hutto. During his lifetime, Carl improved the property greatly and it became one of the prettiest and most valuable in the area. He had three brothers: Ernest, who lived near Round Rock, and two brothers that remained in Sweden. Until his death in 1917, he took an active part in the church work.

Carl married Ida Lax in 1888. Ida was the daughter of a tailor, Carl Lax. She was born in Forserum, Smaland, Sweden in 1863. At the age of twenty, she immigrated to Texas and worked for the Andrew Palm family at Round Rock. Carl and Ida had four children: Elenora, born in 1888, Tom 1890, Carl 1892, and Rosie 1894. Ida had two brothers: John Lax, who lived near Brushy, and a brother who remained in Sweden. Carl died in 1917 and Ida in 1927. Mr. and Mrs. Anderson were charter members of the Swedish Free Church and are buried in the church cemetery.

Carl Anderson family

Carl Anderson, a farmer and homeowner, lived in the Brushy area since his arrival from Sweden. He was born in Malmback parish, Smaland, Sweden in 1857. His parents were Anders and Karin Anderson and in the home were five brothers and sisters. Among them were an older brother named Johan who came to America in 1869, but his whereabouts or destiny was unknown. His remaining siblings stayed in Sweden. Carl worked on the land until 1882 when he traveled to America with Round Rock as his destination. After Carl arrived in Texas, he first worked for Andrew Nelson, and after a few years he leased a farm for thirteen years. In 1901 he bought a farm of 150 acres, which he made improvements such as a house and new barns. He succeeded well in his vocation with his sons who stayed home and helped him on the farm.

In 1887, Carl married Christina Johanson. She was born in 1858 in Raberga, Smaland, Sweden but grew up in Lekeryd, Sweden. Her parents were Johan and Johanna Anderson. In 1885, she immigrated to Texas, where she worked in Georgetown until she married. The couple had six children: Edwin born 1890, John 1892, Ester 1897, Enoch 1900, Hannah 1902, and Oscar 1904. The two oldest sons were among the first men in the area to enlist in the U.S. Army. Carl died in 1946 and Christina in 1943. Mr. and Mrs. Anderson were charter members of the Swedish Free Church and are buried in the church cemetery.

Claus Henning Anderson family

Claus Anderson was born in 1868 and came from Byarum, Smaland, Sweden but moved to Oggestorp, Sweden as a young boy where he grew and received his schooling. He worked on a farm for a while. After fulfilling his army duty, and with royal consent for him to emigrate, Anderson came to America in 1889. His destination was Georgetown. He first found work with Mrs. Jonas Lindell as a farmhand. After two years, he went to Iowa where he stayed and worked around Harcourt. However, Texas weather seemed better and he returned after a few years. He settled in the Brushy Community in 1893 he started to farm, and leased the land. After a few years, he bought a farm of 150 acres.

In 1893, Claus married Josephina Lundholm who he had met in Iowa. Josephine was born in Oggestorp, Smaland, Sweden in 1868. Her father was Johan Lundholm, a tenant farmer at Ulfsnas. In 1891, she arrived in America. Claus and Josephine had six children: Ellen born in 1888, Alice 1895, Fred 1896, Ruth 1898, Alma 1899, Lizzie 1901, and Bill 1903. Claus died in 1947 and Josephine in 1955. Both are buried in the church cemetery.

Claus Ferdinand Anderson family

Claus Anderson immigrated to Round Rock in 1878. His father's brother, Johan Johnson had settled in the vicinity of Georgetown, and Claus worked for him for the first few years. His parent's home was Barkeryd parish, Smaland, Sweden where his father, Anders Johan Danielson, was a tenant farmer. Claus had two brothers: Claus F. August settled in Houston and Johan stayed in Sweden. Claus was born in 1860 and learned at an early age to be a shoemaker. However he didn't practice the craft in Texas, but chose to be a farmer.

In 1888 Claus married Augusta Maria Kvist. She was born in 1861 to August and Johanna Kvist, of Forserum parish, Smaland, Sweden where her father was a soldier. She came to Texas the year prior to her marriage. The couple had three children: Victoria born in 1888, Carl 1890, and Eric 1894.

Mr. Anderson bought his home in 1911. Before that he had leased a farm for over twenty years. Unlike most immigrants, Anderson took three trips to Sweden. He first went back in 1886 and returned to Texas the following year. The second time he took his family with him in 1896 and stayed until 1900. Two years later, the family went again, and stayed for two years until 1904. Claus died in 1929 and Augusta in 1928. Both are buried in the church cemetery.

Carl Gustaf Adolph Anderson family

Carl Gustaf Adolph Anderson was born in 1861 in Sandsjo parish, Smaland, Sweden. His father, Frans Johan Anderson, was a farmer and a shoemaker by profession. Carl had three brothers and four sisters. He left his parent's home in 1882 and immigrated to Round Rock where he worked for Daniel Heard at Chandler Branch. After a few years, he started leasing farms in different places throughout Williamson County. In 1910 Carl bought his own land in the Brushy Community. Later, he exchanged it for another farm near Edna in Jackson County.

In 1887, Carl married Alice Gage. She was born in Live Oak County, Texas in 1869. Her father, Tom Gage, was a fruit dealer. The couple had ten children: Frank born in1888, Anton 1890, Annie 1891, Hulda 1894, Lee 1898, Edna 1901, George 1903, Oscar 1905, Jewel 1908, and Ruby 1912. Carl died in 1944 and Alice in 1946. Both are buried in the church cemetery.

August Anderson family

August Anderson was born in 1863 in Sandsjo parish, Smaland, Sweden where his father, Frans Anderson, was a shoemaker by trade. In his home he received a good education and worked the land. At the age of twenty-two he emigrated from Sweden to try his luck and prove his manhood. In 1885 he arrived in Round Rock where he worked for Herman Stark for three years and was paid monthly wages. After this, he had then saved enough money to be able to lease land. For around 20 years, he farmed other estates in the Brushy area. In 1906, he brought the farm in Berry's Creek, where he and his family lived and worked.

In 1900, August married Amalia Orn. She was born in Brushy, Texas in 1880. Her farther, Gustaf Orn, was a farmer in the area for many years. The Anderson's had four children: Arthur born in 1901, Alma 1902, Ellen 1906, and Evelyn 1912. August had seven siblings and Amalia had six siblings all of whom lived in Texas.

Alex Simon Anderson family

Alex Anderson was born in Mjolby, Ostergotland, Sweden in 1883 to Vilhelm and Matilda Anderson. His father was a miller by trade. In 1903, Alex immigrated to Williamson County, Texas. For the first several years he worked on different farms in the Brushy area. After he had earned enough money, he leased a farm in 1907, and became a tenant farmer in the Berry's Creek Community.

The following year he married Hulda Maria Lax, the daughter of the John and Christina Elizabeth Lax of Brushy where her family had lived for many years. Hulda was born in 1888. She received a good education for life in home, school and church. The couple's children were: Lillian born in1909, Howard 1911, Ethel 1913, Roland 1915,Homer 1917, Irene 1920, Elmer 1922, Laverne 1923, and Edgar 1926. Hulda died in 1945 and Alex died in 1964. They are buried in the church cemetery.

Tom Henry Anderson family

Tom Henry Fengal Anderson, the oldest son of Carl and Ida Anderson, grew up near Georgetown where he received a good education and he chose to be a farmer. In 1913 he married Esther Carlson, the daughter August and Clara Carlson of Brushy. Esther was born and raised in the Brushy Community and lived there all her life. The couple had seven children: Loraine born in1915, Oliver 1917, Ruby Lee 1918, Vivian 1920, Pauline (date unknown), Clarice 1926, and Herbert 1928. Esther died in 1968 and Tom died in 1971. Both are buried in the church cemetery.

Albin E. Blomquist family

Albin Blomquist, a farmer and tenant in the vicinity of Georgetown, was the son of Aron and Edla Blomquist of Berry's Creek. He was born in Williamson County in 1888, and grew up on his father's farm. He leased one of Henry Lundblad's farms between Brushy and Georgetown, where he lived for many years.

In 1909, he married Adina Sandberg, the daughter of Mrs. John Brogren of Berry's Creek (see Brogren family). She was born in Brushy in 1884. The couple had four children:

Morris born in 1910, Albertha 1913, Duval 1915, and Alice 1917.

Johan Ignatius Bergstrom family

Johan Bergstrom was born in Jersnas parish, Smaland, Sweden in 1858. His parents, Gustaf and Maria, were tenant farmers at Sundsholm Estate. Johan left Sweden in 1881 in the company of ten other people from the same area who were also headed for Texas. After Johan arrived, he worked for one of the oldest Swedish pioneers in Williamson County, John Kristerson of Brushy. In 1897, Johan purchased a farm north of Hutto.

In 1883, Johan married Kristina Larson, born in 1859 in Lekeryd, Sweden. They had seven children: Selma born in 1882, Amalia 1885, Dixie 1887, Philip 1890, Henry 1892, Esther and Alice 1894 (the twins died two and three months of age). Kristina died a few months later in January 1895. She and her twins are buried in the church cemetery.

In 1897, Mr. Bergstrom married Mrs. Josephina Anderson. She was from Sodra, Smaland, and had a son, Fingal Anderson from her previous marriage who grew up in the Bergstrom household. Josephine and Johan had one child, Walter born in 1898. Josephine died in 1904.

In 1906, Mr. Bergstrom married Bella Susanna Chellgren. She was born in the Brushy Community in 1883, and raised in the home of her maternal grandfather, Mr. Jacobson of Hutto. The couple had two children: Frances born in 1907 and Harold 1909. Johan died in 1931 and Bella in 1941. They are buried in the church cemetery.

Ture Albert Bergstrom family

Ture Bergstrom was a landowner and farmer in the vicinity of Weir where he owned a beautiful farm of 210 acres. He was born in Jersnils parish, Smaland, Sweden in 1866. His father, Gustaf Johanson, was a wooden shoemaker, a position very much in demand in those days. Ture became so competent in this work before he grew up that he could make twelve pair of shoes in one day. He soon decided to try some other work, so he went to Huskvarna, Sweden where he found a job in a weapons factory. He stayed there for around four years.

In 1885, after a year in Stockholm, Ture immigrated to Texas and worked as a farmhand near Georgetown. He became a tenant farmer and lived in different locations throughout Williamson County for thirteen years. Ture later moved to Weir where he bought his own land in 1901. He succeeded in his work with the help of his children. He also owned a farm in Stonewall County. The family was respected and active in the community and in the work of their church.

In 1889, Ture married Hilda Amanda Gustafson. Hilda was born in Helleberga, Kronoberg, Sweden to Gustaf and Sara Helena Adolphson. She was the youngest of seven children and immigrated to Texas in 1888. Her mother came over for a short visit, but soon returned to Sweden. The couple had eleven children: Bessie born in 1890, Hilding 1891, Rosa 1893, Gustaf 1895, Hilda 1897, Joseph 1899, Martin 1903, Ellen 1904, Anna 1906, Oscar 1908, and Carl 1910. Ture died in 1942 and Hilda in 1961. Both are buried in the church cemetery.

John Adolph Boman family

John Boman came from Ekeby parish, Ostergotland, Sweden where he was born in 1872. His father was a soldier named Bowman. Before John immigrated to Texas, he worked for a few years in the forest (job unknown) and did farm work. When John arrived to Williamson County in 1893 he found work on various farms. About three years later, he leased a farm in the area. In 1900 he purchased 120 acres near Georgetown and turned the land into a beautiful farm.

John married Anna Dahlberg in 1902. She was born in Jersnas parish, Smaland, Sweden in 1876. She came to Manor at the age of eighteen. Before she married, she worked in Georgetown and in Fort Worth. Her parents were Johan and Augusta Dahlberg. Her father was a factory worker in Sweden. After his death, her mother came to Brushy and she died in 1914. Anna had several sisters and brothers in America. Of Mr. Boman's seven brothers and sisters, two stayed in Sweden but the others immigrated to America. The couple had seven children: Elmer born in 1903,Oscar 1904, Bertha 1905, Paul 1907, Deborah 1908, Royal 1909, and Berthel 1913. Johan died in 1961 and Anna in 1967. Both are buried in the church cemetery.

Simon Borg family

Simon Borg was born in Forserum parish, Smaland, Sweden in 1885. He came to Texas at the age of six with his parents, August and Maria Borg, and the rest of his family in 1891. His father was a farmer in Jonah. Simon helped his father on the family farm until 1909. For a few years he leased land in the Jonah area to farm on his own. He then moved to McCulloch County for a short time where he leased land from his father-in-law, but then returned to the Brushy area.

In 1909 he married Mary Elizabeth Carlson from Jonah. She was the daughter of Swen August and Elin Carlson. She was born near Manor, Texas in 1888. She later moved to Jonah with her parents, where she grew up and went to school. There were eight brothers and sisters in her family; she was the oldest. Mary and Simon had four children: William born in 1910, Irma 1911, Kermit 1913, and Irvin 1921. Simon died in 1946 and Mary in 1952. They are buried in Austin Memorial Park Cemetery.

Hans Bostrom family

Hans Bostrom was born in 1851 and emigrated from Sweden in 1878. Han's wife, Annie (last name unknown) was born in 1853, and emigrated the same year as her husband. It is unknown whether they were married, or even knew each other when they left Sweden. However they settled in Kansas for several years before moving to Texas. Mr. and Mrs. Bostrom were charter members of the Swedish Free Church. The couple had five children (the first three were born in Kansas): Oscar 1882, Elma 1883, Frieda 1886, Hannah 1891, and Martin 1894.

Erik John Brogren family

Erik John Brogren, a charter member of the Swedish Free Church, was born in 1855 in Nora, Varmland, Sweden but left when he was nine years old as his parents moved to a farm at Hidinge, Narke, Sweden. Before he came to America in 1885, he worked for several years in factories in Forserum and Kalmar, in the latter he worked as foreman of the factory. Therefore, it was very hard for him to get used to working as a farmer in the hot sun in Texas. He had a job on Mr. Jonas Lindell's farm in Brushy, but decided to go back to Sweden. His old boss in Kalmar paid for his return trip.

After three years in his homeland, he returned to Texas where he went to work for the old pioneer, Jonas Kristerson in Brushy. In 1900 he sold his belongings and went back to Sweden. During this time in Texas, he had been partly a tenant farmer and partly a carpenter. After he came back, he took up the same occupation a few years in Round Rock and a few years in Del Valle. He ran the Swedish owned cotton gin in Round Rock for four years. Later, he moved to Berry's Creek and took up farming. There he owned a beautiful farm in a fertile valley.

In 1893, Erik Brogren married Hanna S. (her last name is unknown). She died nineteen days after their wedding. There is little information as to cause of death or her history. She was the second person buried in the Free Church Cemetery. Erik later married Karin Soderquist from northern Sweden, but she died in 1904 leaving a son, Elliot born in 1900, and a foster daughter, Mildred Mercer. Katerina was also buried in the Free Church Cemetery, however the grave is unmarked.

In 1908, he married Mrs. Anna Christian Sandberg. Anna was born in 1859 in Forserum parish, Smaland, to Sven and Johanna Benjaminson. She came to Texas in the company of her husband, August Sandberg in 1881, and lived in Brushy until he died in 1898. She had two children with her first husband: Adina and Ruben. Anna died in 1927 and John in 1945. Both are buried in the church cemetery.

August Albert Carlson family

August Albert Carlson was born in Vastergotland, Sweden in 1862. His parents, C.O. and Stina Lisa Gustafson, were farmers. At the age of 18, August became a sailor and sailed on Lake Vettern for about two years. But something was pulling at him to journey further from his homeland. In 1883 he arrived in Texas. He first came to Brushy and found work with August Sandberg. He began to make himself at home and became a successful cotton farmer in the Brushy area near the Free Church. He also owed a farm in the Swedish community of Kenedy.

August married Clara Svensson, daughter of Sven Benjaiminson. Clara was born in Forserum, Smaland, Sweden in 1861, and immigrated to America in 1883. She made her way to Texas where she worked in both Georgetown and Austin. The couple had seven children: Philip born in 1886, Agnes 1888, Erik 1891, Esther 1893, Alma1895, Frank 1897, and Gustaf 1902. August died in 1930 and Clara in 1950. Both are buried in the church cemetery.

Carl August Carlson family

Carl August Carlson was born in Texas in 1878. His parents, Otto and Lovisa Carlson, came as immigrants in the first era of immigration and were farmers in Brushy. He received a good education and helped his father on the farm while growing up. On reaching maturity, he chose the same occupation. For many years he was a tenant farmer in the area. Carl's sister, Hulda Carlson, married Carl Emil Anderson.

In 1902, Carl married Hulda Swenson, daughter of Oscar Swenson. Hulda was also born in the Brushy area in 1883. Her parents came to this country in the early years and settled in Williamson County. She had two brothers, Walter and Swen, also half sisters, Ruth and Mabel and half brothers, Eric and Hilmer. Carl and Hulda had four children: Oscar born in 1903, Evelyn 1906, John 1909, and Walter 1911.

Philip Carlson family

Philip Carlson, the oldest son of August and Clara Carlson, was born in 1886. He leased his father's farm and had his own land in the Kenedy settlement. He went to public school and also took a course at Griffith's Business College in Austin.

In 1910, Philip married Ruth Lawson the daughter of John J. Lawson of Brushy. She was born in 1887. The couple had one child, Jeanette born in 1916. Ruth died in 1932 and Philip in 1970. Both are buried in the church cemetery.

Swen August Carlson family

Swen August Carlson was born in Traheryd, Smaland, Sweden in 1858. His father was Carl J. Carlson, a carpenter. Swen was a miller in Sweden, but after he immigrated to Texas in 1883 he became a farmer in the Jonah Colony.

In 1884 Swen married Elin Lindberg, the same year she emigrated from Sweden. She was born in Gryts parish, Kristianstad in 1862. Her father, M.E. Lindberg was a night guard at the estate in Varnas. Although the couple lived in Jonah they were members of the Swedish Free Church in Brushy. The couple had eight children: Emil born in 1887, Mary Elizabeth 1888, Maud 1891, Edith 1893 Leonard 1895, unnamed infant 1897, Ellen 1900, and Ethel 1905. Elin died in 1937 and Swen in 1947. Both are buried in the church cemetery.

Carl Ekdahl family

Carl Ekdahl was born in Vanga, Vastergotland, Sweden in 1867. He immigrated to Georgetown in 1891. He worked for three years for Mr. Oscar Forsvall, then leased land, and a farm in 1905. He married Anna Johnson in 1897. She was born in Wallsjo, Smaland, Sweden in 1876. She immigrated to Texas in 1896. The couple had six children: Gunner born in 1898, Oscar 1900, Emil 1902, Wesley 1907, Mildred 1909, and Juliet 1917. Carl died in 1938 and Anna in 1960. Both are buried in the church cemetery.

John Alfred Eklund family

John Alfred Eklund was born in 1866 in Skaraborg, Sweden. He grew up in the country and learned to farm in his homeland. His parents were Johannes and Maria Anderson. There were five children in the family among whom John and his sister, Christina (Mrs. Oscar Swenson of Thrall), came as immigrants to Texas in 1889. He found work in the Brushy area as a farmhand for Carl Anderson for whom he worked a couple of years. He bought a farm in 1899 located along the Georgetown-Round Rock highway.

John married Kristina Forsvall in 1890. She was born in Odestugu parish, Smaland, Sweden in 1855. She immigrated to Texas in 1884. Her parents, who were farmers, later came to Texas where they died in Brushy. Kristina had one sister, Augusta, and a brother, Oscar that also came to Texas. John and Kristina had five children (three of whom died) Paul born 1896, and Minnie born in 1898. John died in 1949 and is buried in the church cemetery. The date in which Kristina died is unknown, and her remains rest in a unmarked grave in the church cemetery. Mr. and Mrs. Eklund were charter members of the church.

Carl Johan Ekvall family

Carl Johan Ekvall, born in 1857, was from Ostergotland, Sweden. His father, Per Oscar Forsman, was a shoemaker and Carl learned the trade. In 1879 Carl married Hanna W. Jacobson. Hanna was born in the same region as Carl in 1856. The couple had five children; Karl born in 1880, Joe 1883, Lydia 1888, Olof 1891, and Frida 1894. In 1903 the Carl Ekvall family immigrated to Texas where he became a farmer. Carl died in 1936 and Hanna in 1940. Both are buried in the St. John's United Methodist Cemetery.

Anders Johan Engvall family

Anders Engvall was born in Balaryd parish, Jonkoping, Sweden in 1869. His father, S.A. Johnson, was a farmer. He immigrated to America in 1887. He worked on S. M. Swenson's sugar plantation in Louisiana before coming to Texas. He purchased a farm in the Georgetown area in 1906.

In 1894, Anders married Mrs. Hanna Kylberg. She was born in 1868 and was the daughter of Mrs. Rebecka Lundblad and her late husband. The family came to Texas when Hanna was two years old. Hanna had a daughter, Ellen, with her husband August Kylberg. Anders and Hanna had five children: August 1897, Sven 1902, Lillian 1908, Floyd 1911, and Rosalie 1918.

Alfred John Gilberg family

Alfred Gilberg, the oldest son of John A. and Johanna Gilberg, was born in Austin, Texas, in 1878. His parents, some of the first Swedish settlers in central Texas, were farmers. Alfred helped his father until he started out on his own. He purchased land in the Swedish Community of Berry's Creek in 1907. Alfred married Annie Orn in 1900. She was born in Palm Valley in 1876. Her father, Gustaf Orn, was one of the early pioneers and later settled in Williamson County. Annie was one of seven children, most of whom stayed in the area. Alfred and Annie had two children: Mabel born in 1901, and Lawrence 1902.

Carl H. Gustafson family

Carl Gustafson, son of Gustaf Johson, was from Barkeryd parish, Smaland, Sweden where he was born in 1867. In 1883, he immigrated to Texas where he worked on farms in the Round Rock area for several years before becoming a landowner and farmer. He was one of the twenty-three charter members of the Brushy Free Church.

In 1896 Carl married Emma Carolina Dyk, whose parents home was in Ahnesakra, Smaland, Sweden. She immigrated to Texas in 1887. The couple had four children: Annie and Lillie born in 1896, Naomi 1898, and Ellen 1900. Emma died in 1924 and Carl in 1932. Both are buried in the church cemetery.

Carl G. Holmstrom family

Carl G. Holmstrom, born in Jonkoping, Sweden in 1869, was the son of Per Johan Johanson, a farmer and a carpenter. Before Carl immigrated to Texas in 1888, he was also a farmer and a miller in Sweden. Once Carl arrived in Texas, he worked for Mr. Carl Lundgren of Decker, worked two years in Austin, and then moved to Williamson County where he was a tenant farmer for twelve years. In 1904 he had bought a beautiful farm in the near the Jonah Colony on the San Gabriel River, and moved his family there the following year.

In 1894 Carl married Anna Sofia Frojd, daughter of Anders Frojd. She was born in Almesakra, Smaland, Sweden in 1872, and immigrated to

America in 1891, and came to Round Rock in the company of the widow Lovisa Peterson of Taylor.

Mr. Holmstrom was a cheerful and friendly person who made friends early both among Swedes and Americans. He took a great part in community activities, and was a representative for the Jonah public schools for several years. He was also part owner of a local gin company. A paternal uncle of Mr. Holmstrom, Gustaf Holmstrom, came here before the Civil War, and afterwards he settled in Minnesota where he died at an old age. The couple had seven children: Oscar born in 1895, Gustaf 1897, Tom 1901, Bertha 1903, Lambert 1905, Walter 1907, and Frances 1909. Anna died in 1940 and Carl died in 1949. Both are buried in the Taylor City Cemetery.

Andrew Johnson family

Andrew Johnson came to Texas with his parents, Johannes and Katarina Israelson in 1878, when he was nine years old. He helped his father with the farm work until he bought his own farm near the Hutto Colony in 1893. His parents lived with him in their later years and they both died in his home. Andrew married Anna Anderson in 1896. She was born in Malmback, Sweden where she emigrated from in 1886. The couple has two children: Paul 1897 and Esther 1901.

Axel Johnson family

Axel Johnson was born in 1887, and emigrated from Smaland, Sweden in 1906. He first came to Round Rock and then lived in the Jonah Colony where he began a cotton farmer. Axel married Linnea (last name unknown) who was also from Smaland. She was born in 1895, and she came to Texas seven years after Axel. They married soon after her arrival. The couple had two children: Sidne 1914 and Margaret 1916.

Carl H. Johnson family

Carl Johnson was born in 1860 and grew up on a farm in Lekeryd parish, Smaland, Sweden. He received his education in a parish school. His father, J.T. Swenson was a carpenter, and his mother was Maria Katarina. In Sweden, Johnson worked the land for his father, but when he became of age he started thinking about Texas, which was well-known in Smaland. At the age of twenty-three, and after he had completed military service, Johnson left his homeland to seek his fortune in a foreign land. He set out for Texas and Round Rock as his destination. His parents and four siblings also immigrated to America. When Johnson first came to Texas, he worked for Mr. Newlin in the Brushy area and then for several years he worked on different farms. He leased land and after four years he bought his own farm in Brushy Colony in 1898.

Carl married Hannah Johnson in 1892. She was born in 1870 also in Smaland. She emigrated from Sweden in 1890 and stayed with the Henry Lundblad family near Georgetown. Later she worked in town until she married. Her four siblings also immigrated to this country. Hanna died in 1938 and Carl died in 1960, both are buried in the church cemetery. The couple had no children.

Johan Alfred Johnson family

Alfred Johnson was born in Smaland, Sweden in 1871 to Johan and Johanna Anderson. He immigrated to Texas in 1890, and worked for his brother-in-law, Carl Anderson, for a year near Georgetown; there he earned his first dollar. He then leased land and after twelve years, he bought his own farm in the Berry's Creek area.

In 1894, Johan married Hulda Orn. She was born in 1874 in Brushy, also a homeowner in the Swedish Community of Berry's Creek. She was the daughter of Gustaf and Augusta Orn, who were early pioneers in this area. Alfred and Hulda had eight children, (one daughter died and is not listed): Ellen born in 1895, Carl 1897, Nora 1901, Walter 1904, Hannah 1906, Irene 1909 and Maurice 1912.

Gustaf Johnson family

Gustaf Johnson was trained to be a shoemaker, but he left that profession and came to Texas in 1893, a year known for hard times and difficult job opportunities. Around Round Rock, young Johnson worked as a farm hand and soon became a tenant farmer. After eight years, he went back to his old home in Sandsjo, Smaland, Sweden where he had been born in 1873. When Gustaf returned to Texas in 1902, he was a married man in the company of the wife, Hilma Victoria Johnson. Her home was in Nassjo, and her father, Johan Johnannesson, was a farmer. She was born in 1880.

When Johnson returned to Texas, he bought a farm near Jonah, which he improved and renovated as one of the most beautiful in the colony. Mr. Johnson and others Swedes in Jonah mostly grew cotton. The couple had five children: Elvira born in1904, Sigurd 1905, Hildur 1908, Irma 1911, and Sven Jonah 1916. Gustaf had seven siblings, five of which came to America. Hilma had four siblings in this country and four who remained in Sweden.

Gustaf Edward Johnson family

Gustaf Edward Johnson was born in Jersnas parish, Smaland, Sweden in 1863. His parents were Johan and Lovisa Jansson, and he grew up on their farm, learning early how to run a farming business. He emigrated from his homeland in 1883 to Texas. He worked for Henry Lundblad, near Georgetown, for the first five years. Then he leased one of the farms for an additional three years. He had been counted as a landowner since 1890, because he bought land together with Carl Gustafson. After several years he sold his share to Gustafson and first bought a smaller place in the same area, then a larger one which he built up and improved with modern buildings. When the Swedish Community of Lyford started he also became interested in the venture and bought some land there. Johnson was a good farmer and devoted himself mostly to raising cotton.

In 1893 Gustaf married Anna Anderson. She was born in 1874 and came to Texas in 1891 and lived in Georgetown. Her parents, Anders and Martha Anderson, were farmers and lived in Oggestrop parish, Smaland. She had five siblings. The couple had seven children: Minnie born in 1895, Beda 1897, Joseph 1899, Gustaf 1900, Nora 1903, Wesley 1907, and Martin 1910.

Oscar Johnson family

Oscar Johnson was born in 1876, where his father, Johannes Jonason, was a tenant farmer on the church land in Smaland, Sweden. Johnson was one of six children, four of whom immigrated to America. Oscar immigrated to Texas in 1896, and was a tenant farmer in Brushy before he became a cattle buyer and trader. In 1902 Oscar married Agda Dahlberg, who was born in 1878 in Jersnas, Smaland. The couple had two children, Grace born in 1906 and Morris born in 1910.

Johannes Julius Lawson (Larson) family

Johannes Julius Lawson was born in Jersnas, Smaland, Sweden in 1857. He belonged to the old well-known Kristerson family as his father, Lars Kristerson, was a brother of Jonas Kristerson, one of the first Swedish settlers in Texas. His uncle had come here with this family probably in 1854, before the Civil War. Lawson came to his uncle's home in 1879 and worked for two years. He then purchased his own farm in the Brushy Colony.

In 1887 Johannes married Adla Susanna, born in 1858 in Williamson Country. Their infant daughter, Pearl, born in 1889, died three months after her birth and was the first person buried at the Free Church Cemetery. Other children were: Ruth 1887, Ben 1892, Birdie 1894, Hilda 1895, and Julius 1898. Mr. Lawson was a charter member of the Swedish Free Church. Alda died in 1911 and Johannes in 1940. Both are buried in the church cemetery.

John Lax family

John Lax was born in Fintorp in 1860, but came from Forserum parish, Smaland, Sweden. His father, Carl Johan Lax, was a tailor by trade, but John did farm work and stayed in that occupation until he immigrated to America. In 1881 John left his homeland and began the journey to the vast land of Texas, where so many for his countrymen from Smaland had gone. When he arrived in Round Rock, he worked for Andrew Palm to pay off his passage. He was a tenant farmer in Williamson County for nineteen years before he bought his farm in 1905. He built a modern home and barns, resulting in one of the prettiest farmers in the area. He also owned land in the Swedish Community of Lyford.

In 1885, John married Christina Elizabeth Holmstrom, who immigrated to Texas the year prior. Her parents, Per Johan and Elizabeth Johannson, were from Gransang Farm, Barkeryd parish, Smaland, where she was born in 1865. Of the four children in her family, only Christina and her brother, Carl Holmstrom (who lived in Jonah) immigrated to Texas.

John and Christina had seven children: Anna born in 1886, Hulda 1888, Henry 1890, Eric 1892, Mabel 1898, Arthur 1900, and Edith 1903. Mr. and Mrs. Lax were charter members of the Swedish Free Church. John lax died in 1918 and Elizabeth in 1931. Both are buried in the church cemetery.

Philip Lind family

Philip Lind's childhood home was Harlunda parish, Vastergotland, Sweden where he was born in 1880. His father, A.G. Lind, was a tenant farmer. Philip had ten siblings, among which two brothers and a sister came to America. His sister, Maria lived in Oakland, California. Philip immigrated to Texas in 1901. He learned his blacksmith trade in his homeland and when he came to Williamson County he worked for William Sandgren, a master blacksmith, where he stayed there for eleven years. In 1912, Philip was among the first Swedish businessmen and professionals in Georgetown. He started his own wheelwright and blacksmith shop which developed and prospered. Philip was a man of many talents. One of his early inventions was shock absorbers for Model T Fords which he manufactured and marketed.

Philip married Esther Dahlberg in 1907. She was born in Forserum parish, Smaland, in 1883. Her parents were Johan and Augusta Dalhberg. She left her homeland and came to America in 1904. She worked in Austin and Georgetown before her marriage. The couple had three children, Richard, born in 1908, Edna, 1913, and Lawrence 1919. Her mother came to Texas, where she died in 1914. Esther died in 1919. Both mother and daughter are buried in the Free Church Cemetery. Shortly after Esther's death, Philip married Anna Elizabeth Lax Peterson, the widow of Carl Peterson. Philip died in 1957 and Anna in 1958. Both are buried in the church cemetery.

Claus Lindquist family

Claus Lindquist was born in Svenarum, Smaland, where he was both a farmer and a factory worker. In 1897, he immigrated to Texas. He leased land and then purchased his own farm. Claus married Anna C. Adolfson in 1903. She came to Texas with her parents in 1886 when she was three years old. The couple had four children: Arnold born 1904, Weldon 1907,

Howard 1910, and Irene 1920. Most of the members of this family are buried in the church cemetery.

Henry Nord family

Henry Nord was born in Forserum, Smaland, Sweden in 1865 to Mr. and Mrs. Claus Joahanson. Henry immigrated to Texas in 1888 where he was a tenant farmer before buying land in 1907. He married Jenny Johnson in 1892. She was born in 1869, the daughter of Adam Jonsson, a tailor in Kulltorp, Smaland. She immigrated to Texas in 1890. The couple had eight children: Ellen born in 1893, Oscar 1895, Paul 1897, Esther 1899, Naomi 1902, Florence 1904, Wesley and Lillian 1909. Jenny died in 1915 and Henry in 1952. Both are buried in the church cemetery.

Will Nord family

Will Nord was born in Forserum, Smaland, Sweden in 1870, to Mr. and Mrs. Claus Joahanson. He immigrated to Texas in 1891. He was a carpenter and farmer by trade. In the 1908 census report, it states that he owned 109 acres. Will married Annie Marie Sund in1892. Annie Marie was born in Forserum, Smaland, Sweden in 1874. Will and Annie Marie Sund immigrated to America on the same ship, but it is unknown if they knew each other before departing. The couple had eleven children: Minnie born in1893, Ellen 1893, Elenora 1896, Rose 1898, Elmer 1900, Hadley 1901, Naomi 1903, Ethel 1905, Ruben 1907, Myrtle 1909, and Alvin 1911. Annie Marie Nord died in 1918 and buried in the church cemetery.

In 1922, Will married Lizzie Jansen Schneider, the widow of Alfred Schneider. She was born in 1887. Lizzie and Alfred had four children: Edger born in 1906, William 1908, Max 1910, and Ben 1912. Will and Lizzie had three children: Lula born in 1924, Viola 1926, and Lee Roy1927. Will died in 1953 and Lizzie died in 1972. They are buried in the church cemetery.

Carl Gideon Peterson family

Carl Gideon Peterson, son of Sven Peterson, was born in 1887 in Barnarp parish, Smaland, Sweden, but came to Texas with his parents at the age of three months. He grew up in the Brushy area and lived there until he moved to the Taylor area. In 1916, he married Anna Elizabeth Lax, the daughter of John Lax, of Brushy. She was born in 1886 in McNeil, Texas. They took an active role in the youth organization of the church. The couple had one child, Anne Belle born in 1918. That same year Carl died after being struck by lightning, and is buried in the church cemetery.

John Peterson family

John Peterson Jr., the son of John Peterson, a tailor in Hutto, was born in Kansas City, Missouri in 1886. At the age of eleven, he moved to Texas with his parents. His family first settled in Victoria County and later moved to Williamson County. John became a tenant farmer and lived near Georgetown. In 1910 he married Ellen Kylberg, who was born in the Brushy Colony of Williamson County in 1889. They had one son, John Roy born in 1913.

Sven Peterson family

Sven Peterson was born in the Barnarp parish, Smaland, Sweden in 1857. His parents, Per Johan and Kristina Johanneson were farmers. Sven was also a farmer until he emigrated in 1887. His wife, Augusta Marie Frisk, and their oldest son Gideon, who was only a few weeks old, emigrated with him. When the family arrived in Texas, they settled in Williamson County, except between 1890-1893, when they lived in Decker.

Sven and Augusta married in1886. She was born in 1856, and her home was in Lekeryd parish where her father, Johan Frisk was a soldier in the Jonkoping Royal Regiment. The couple had seven children: Gideon born in 1887, Emmie 1888, Ruth 1890, Edith 1892, Gustaf 1894, Hulda 1895, and Simon 1897.

John Rosenblad family

John Rosenblad was born in Stockholm, Sweden in 1872, but grew up in Taby parish where he went to school. His father was a shoemaker by trade. When the John left his homeland in 1892, his destination was the Brushy Colony in Williamson County. Like most Swedes, he came to Texas as a poor emigrant to work off his passage, and then for monthly wages. He managed through hard work and thrift to save enough money to start his own farm. He leased land for two years until he bought a farm in 1902. He organized the Bell Gin Company in 1913, which built a cotton gin near the Bell schoolhouse, not far from his home in the Brushy Colony. Mr. Rosenblad had three sisters who remained in Sweden.

In 1895, John married Anna Setterlof, born in the Kumla parish, Narke, in 1870. Her parents, P.E. and Sofia Setterlof, were tenant farmers. She immigrated to America in1893, first to Brooklyn, N.Y. where she stayed for one year before coming to Texas. The couple had seven children: Rhoda born in1896, Joseph 1898, Ben 1900, Ruben 1902, Tom 1905, John 1907 and Lawrence 1911(abt). Anna died in 1947 and John in 1948. They are buried in the church cemetery.

J. August Sandburg family

August Sandburg was born in 1857. He and his wife, Anna Christine Svensson, emigrated from Sweden in 1881. The couple had three children: Hilda born in 1882, Adina 1884, and Rueben 1891. Mr. and Mrs. Sandburg were charter members of the Swedish Free Church. August died in 1898 and is buried in the church cemetery. Ten years after her husband's death, Anna married Erik Brogren (also a charter member of the church). See Brogren for more information.

Ernest Alex Wolander family

Alex, born in 1872, was from Normlosa, Ostergotland. He immigrated to America in 1890, and married Ida Johnson in 1896. The couple had eight children: Alma 1895, Signe 1898, Mabel 1901, Gunner 1904, Rosie 1905, Carl 1908, Wesley 1911, and Milton 1914. Axel died in 1915 and is buried in the church cemetery.

After her husband's death, Ida ran the farm, which she leased a few miles from Georgetown with the help from her children. Ida was born in Wood County Texas in 1877, but came to Williamson County (after the death of her father) at the age of two with her mother, Anna Johnson. Her parents emigrated from Dalarna in 1873. They went to Norfolk, Virginia before coming to Texas. Ida died in 1969 and is buried in the church cemetery beside her husband.

Carl Oscar Youngbloom family

Carl Youngbloom was one of the twenty-three charter members of the Swedish Free Church. He was born in 1864 in Svarttorpsbo, Smaland, Sweden, but grew up in Hogstorp, Smaland. His father, Johan Blom, was a farmer. Carl emigrated from Hogstorp in 1884 at the age of twenty. His first residence in Texas was in the home of Ludvig Johnson where he found rest after the long journey. He worked for Enoch Johnson for around three years, and then started his own farm as a tenant farmer on the Dimmitt estate near Georgetown. In 1900, Youngbloom purchased some land, but he later sold it and bought a 220 acre farm near Hutto.

In 1888, Carl married Christina Johnson from the Lekeryd parish, Smaland, where she was born in 1858. She came to Texas in 1882. Her parents, who later came to the Brushy Colony were J.T. Svenson, a carpenter, and his wife Maria Katarina. Besides Christina, the Svenson's had four other children here. Carl and Christina had seven children: Wesley born in 1890, Philip 1892, Ellen 1893, George 1895, Rosie 1897, Naomi 1898, and Elna 1900. Carl died in 1935 and Christina in 1945. Both are buried in the church cemetery.

Philip Natanael Youngbloom family

Philip Youngbloom, the second son of Carl O. Youngbloom, was born in Georgetown in 1892. Besides a public school education, Philip attended Trinity College in Round Rock. He became a farmer and leased one of his father's farms close to his parents' home. He married Alice Anderson in 1914. She was born in the Brushy Colony in 1895. Her parents were Claus H. Anderson and Josephine Lundholm. Philip and Alice had a daughter, Ora Mae Hortence born in 1916. Philip died in 1976 and Alice in 1987. Both are buried in the church cemetery.

Wesley Youngbloom family

Wesley Youngbloom, the oldest son of Carl O. Youngbloom, was born in 1890 close to Georgetown. He went to public school and stayed in his parent's home until he leased land and started out on his own in 1910. That same year, he married Ellen Anderson. She was born in 1888 to Mr. and

Mrs. C.E. Anderson of the Brushy Colony. She also had a good education and upbringing in school, home, and church. Their four children are: Gladys born in 1912, Edward 1914, Alvin 1916, and Blanche 1917.

Footnote: This chapter was the hardest for me to assemble for this project. Most of the information about the early pioneers of the Brushy Evangelical Free Church were submitted by the family in the early 1900s for the book, *Swedes in Texas In Words and Pictures*. When possible, I left the some of the details as originally published. For additional research such as deaths and births, I used the Swedes in America website (formerly Swedes in Texas) founded by David Borg the grandson of Simon Borg who is mentioned in this section. Unfortunately, I was not able to locate any information about Mr. and Mrs. Carl Bjork who were also charter members of the church. However, I did discover that he was a farmer in the Brushy Colony and his daughter, Ida Charlotta Bjork, married August Hammar of Hutto in 1910. Also please except my apology for any misspellings or other incorrect facts.

I Remember When

The following quotes are memories of long time worshippers who attended the Brushy Church.

I remember:

"looking forward to Vacation Bible School every summer. In the beginning VBS lasted two weeks. We would carpool with neighboring families which was fun." Katherine Nord Stand

"the Christmas programs, and having to recite Christmas speeches in front of the congregation—scary. I was the last to get married in the church on the hill." Ruth Poole

"Georgetown very clearly. It was very hot and there was a dust storm. It was the summer of 1951. I can remember the first time I had ice tea and all the glasses clinking as people stirred their tea. We had never had iced tea before." Enid Anderson Olson

"going to *Jul Otte* Service and singing the song *'Var Halsad Skona Morgonstund'* and other Christmas songs." Thelma Borg

"the chandelier in the Mission Church made out of wire and in two rows—the upper row set in from the lower row. The lights on them were white candles." Gunner Ekdahl

"the Christmas of 1944, our second year in Brady. Coming to Austin for Christmas celebration, there was snow on the mountains and it was so pretty." Ethel Erlanson

"when we had Vacation Bible School at the Bell schoolhouse. Me and Charles Johnson rode bicycles to the Bell School. We rode from CR 116 to CR 111 and took CR 110. That was before they moved the school to the back of the church as a hall." Vermin Eklund

"in the country church building, there were the words 'Be still and know that I am God' written across the front of the church. When I was old enough to read I would sit in the pew next to my parents and ponder what that meant." Katherine Nord Strand

"the Christmas of 1971. We were recently married and this was to be our first Christmas together. I had a job, but was laid off from work. I sold an SHS enemy rifle captured while I was in service in Vietnam for $50.00 in order to buy Christmas presents." Dave Harris

"the Christmas of 1970 at Fort Leonard Wood, Missouri. I was excited about the Christmas Eve service that I had planned. It was my first Christmas Eve service ever as a chaplain and as a minister. We arrived, Linda was ready to play the piano and I was ready to preach. But no one showed up. I couldn't believe it! No one showed up!" Gary Sanford

"the Christmas of 1979 was the first meaningful Christmas I had. We four (Carvin, John, Rachel and me) were home alone on Christmas Eve and Christmas Day; we stayed in Round Rock. We went to a candlelight service on Christmas Eve. The next morning we got up—the kids lit a candle and sang 'Happy Birthday' to Jesus. Then we opened presents. There was no rush to open gifts and there were only a few gifts." Janis Youngbloom

"the country church didn't have air conditioning. Hand held paper fans were provided by local funeral homes." Katherine Nord Strand

"Christmas caroling on Christmas Eve morning. We started at 4 or 5 a.m. and we would go on a hayride either on a trailer or in the back of a pickup or truck. We would go to shut-ins and to anyone who wanted us to come. It was cold. If invited in, we went in. One year we had a progressive breakfast—coffee at one place, cereal in another, and then ended up at the parsonage having bacon and eggs." Irene Lindquist

"my first Christmas speech. I was just a little guy in short pants and said my speech in Swedish, 'I am just a little boy and I wished everyone a Merry Christmas'. However, instead of saying everyone, 'alla', I said 'Lala', which was my cousin's name." Wilbert Johnson

"the Sunday school annual picnics at the San Gabriel Park. Each child was given two tickets for free ice cream or sodas, and homegrown and homemade food was so delicious." Rhoda Ann Ryden Lind

"when I was a child, we lived close to Grandpa, and we would go to his house for Christmas every year, and one of my uncles was Santa Claus. We sang carols and the Christmas treat was Jell-O with whipped topping." Loraine Ekdahl

"when missionaries were on furlough, they would came and speak and show slides of their mission work in Africa." Angeline Nord Cassens

"Johannes Julius Larson. After he came to Texas, he joined the group that was called, 'The Free,' but it was his love for God and his Savior, Jesus Christ, that was his motive. His zeal for the church was untiring. He felt bad if he had to spend anything on himself. He felt as though he was robbing God, and God's work would be slowed down because of him. Before the great revival of 1896, a man in the church had a great revelation. This man was told by the Spirit that the Lord was going to do great things in Brushy. When Brother Larson heard this, he said he knew it because he carried fifty souls before the Throne of Grace every night. He was not a speaker of any sort, but he could pray as few men could." John Rosenblad Sr.

"making cheese. Every year in the fall, farmers would donate fresh milk and the women would gather at the parsonage to make cheese. This was a gift to the pastor." Irene Lindquist "going home from the first Christmas program, I told my mother and father that three names were speaking—actually three older girls had a dialogue." Oscar Ekhahl

"being so loved by everyone at the church." Edith Carlson Layton

"a tradition in the Free Church was confirmation when you reached a certain age. Our teacher was Pastor Rosene and what a 'wild' class of youngsters he had to teach. In our class there were three girls and four boys who attended a class every Saturday for a year. Finally, one Sunday we were brought before the church congregation and answered questions brought by the pastor. After that we were considered 'confirmed' and presented a Bible and diploma by the church. We girls wore white dresses." Natalie Rosenblad Johnson Pascoe

"that I loved the parsonage in the country with warm to hot breezes that blew through our non-air-conditioned home. Hanging clothes on the clothes line after washing them in the wringer washer on the back porch." Karen Thorne Strand

"the corn drive. The congregation collected corn from all the famers that attended the church. The corn was sold and money went toward the church budget." Carvin Youngbloom

"the smorgasbords. I served *dricka* (homemade root beer) and would refill patrons drinks at the tables. It was fun and work at the same time. The tables, 12 foot long boards on saw horses, were set up in the preacher's front yard and the chairs were the folding kind. The ladies from the church made all the food. Everything was homemade. Three hundred to four hundred people were served. Everyone pulled together for this event. It was always successful." Barbara Anderson Johnson

"riding in a buggy to the Christmas Eve program. I had my piece to say and the treat afterward was a sack of candy and an orange. There was a big tree with lighted candles on it and two trustees would stand by with long poles with wet sponges on them to put out sparks." Anna Nord

"learning to drive—practicing driving around the church and the annex." Karen Thorne Strand

"Carl Johan Monson. He was a Godly man, a faithful man, and God blessed him with many earthly goods. He was a very rich man, but he was longing and looking for a better land. In his home among his children, his servants, and others, he was always the same. Prayers and Scripture readings were never forgotten. On Thanksgiving Day, he would have his renters, his servants, and his family together for a great harvest festival." John Rosenblad Sr.

"the men still wore suits and the ladies wore nice dresses, hats, and gloves. Everyone wore their nicest clothes called 'Sunday clothes' to church. When you came home from church, you changed into play clothes or everyday clothes." Carolyn Johnson

"sermons spoken in Swedish one Sunday per month and the dilemma created when the Swedish services were temporarily discontinued. The statement, 'Oh yes, it's on trial basis but the Swedish service will never come back,' became fact." Rhoda Ann Ryden Lind

"the old church and the choir singing, and, especially Evelyn Johnson's father, Oscar Berglund singing the 'Bethlehem Star'." John Rosenblad
"that the ladies sat on one side of the church and the men on the other side. This was how the adults were divided into their Sunday school class, and when the worship service started no one moved. I remember asking, 'When someone dies, are the men and women buried in different parts of the cemetery too'." Irene Lindquist

"Irene Lindquist who faithfully played the organ every Sunday for over sixty years." Joy Nord

"the ladies making root beer and cheese. And Natalie's mother making prune whip." Enid Anderson Olson

"Tom Anderson dropping me and a bunch of other kids off at VBS. Tom would drive into Georgetown and then pick us up on his way home.

And he always tossed us a bag of Orange Slices that he'd bought." Carvin Youngbloom

"on Thanksgiving night was the Harvest Festival. After the program, there were refreshments of delicious pies, coffee and fellowship. Most of the congregation were farmers, so this was an appropriate time of the year for giving." Angeline Nord Cassens

"memorizing speeches, poems and verses. Each class had a verse to memorize." Darrell Ekdahl

"Saturday confirmation classes and the Sunday morning graduation finale in May. Each graduate received a Bible from the church. Shortly after, there was the studio portrait of the class with the guys and girls wearing boutonnieres and corsages made by talented women of the church from Annie and Naomi Gustafson's homegrown sweet peas." Rhoda Ann Ryden Lind

"when I was three years old, I sang at the Manda Methodist Church Christmas program. The song was 'O, How I love Jesus'. There were no gifts for me so afterward I went to the home of the superintendent and got mine." Selma Ekdahl

"that I cried when my first pastor left for another pastorate. At 10 years of age, I didn't know that happened." Carvin Youngbloom

"Nels Jacobson. He worked his land for six years. On the seventh year, he rested. When all the storehouses and barns were full, a year of rest started for his people and his animals. Where other farmers used two horses or mules to pull cultivators, he used four. He seemed to enjoy applying the law of gentleness to everything, and at every meal he would have Scripture reading and prayer." John Rosenblad Sr.

"Gustaf Johnson was a great minister. Many a person came to him and poured out their hearts, and he would console them, give them new hope, pray for them, urge them to renew faith and to believe, hope, pray, and live. Even in later years when he visited our state, elderly men could be seen with their arms around him and their heads on his shoulders weeping." John Rosenblad Sr.

"on the southwest entrance to the old church, there was a water hydrant. By it was a glass holder with a glass in it. If you got thirsty you just rinsed out the glass and got you a drink of water. You put the glass back so someone else could use it." Richard Nord.

"the Women's Ministry was the second Wednesday night of each month. While the mother's were having their meeting, us kids would go play in the cemetery and try to scare each other." Carvin Youngbloom

Swedish Traditions, Smorgasbord, and Harvest Festival

When Swedish immigrants came to Texas, they brought with them many legends, customs, and traditions. Two of their favorites were *Midsommer Dag*, the year's longest day, and *God Jul*, meaning Merry Christmas and a Happy New Year. Once the Swedes were here, they also established new traditions: the *Smorgasbord* and the Harvest Festival. Although one may find some of the Swedish traditions a little weird, especially the Christmas activities, the culture still remains embedded in the hearts of those with a Scandinavian heritage in and around Williamson County.

Midsommer Dag was held during the middle of June to celebrate the arrival of summertime. Festive dancing and joyous singing were featured around maypoles with flower garlands and colorful ribbons. The celebration lasted until nightfall. However, after the Swedes had lived in Texas a few years, they realized that the arrival of summer in Texas wasn't the same *calendar time* as that of their homeland. Here families could pack picnics and head out to the park or countryside much sooner. The celebration was changed to May and became known as Mayfest.

Among the Swedes, *God Jul* was an eagerly anticipated season and full of traditions. Festivities began on December 13, the Day of Lucia and continued non-stop until January 13. The Santa Lucia celebration initiated the start of the Yuletide season. Saint Lucia, a Christian saint, lived in 300 A.D. in Italy and helped the needy. She was imprisoned for her generous acts and cruelly tortured by having her eyes gouged out. To top it all off, she was burned at the stake. Miraculously, Lucia survived. Her death came when she was pierced by a magical sword. After her death she became revered as a saint.

In Swedish households, the eldest daughter portrayed St. Lucia and honored her family by serving them sweet rolls and coffee in the morning. Her attire traditionally consisted of a long white robe tied with a red sash. She wore a metal crown decorated with green sprigs intertwined with red berries. Arranged among the greenery were seven white candles. When lit, they magically transformed the crown into a glowing halo. Although the Saint Lucia tradition no longer takes place among Swedish households here in Texas, the tradition is still upheld by many in Sweden.

Lucia means light in Latin. Saint Lucia, portrayed in art and in celebrations, always carries a torch and wears her crown of lights. Therefore the candles not only represent her name, but what she symbolizes: benevolence, charity, and good fortune.

Another custom that brightened Swedish households during the holidays was *Ljusets Hogtid,* Festival of Lights. Families would light candles in every room to bestow the feelings of warmth, cheer, and the overall Christmas spirit. A candle was also placed in the window as a sign of welcome.

The Christmas tree was set up two days before Christmas and decorated in seasonal spirit with gingerbread biscuits, flowers (poinsettias, red tulips, and red and white amaryllis), candles, ornaments, and tinsel. Fortunately the candle custom was extinguished after a few homesteads went ablaze, which started prairie fires. The flower custom died also, due to unavailable product in the 1800s.

Traditionally Christmas Eve, known as *Julafton*, was celebrated with a large family dinner (*smorgasbord*) with ham, pork, or fish, as well as a variety of sweets. Dessert included a rice pudding with an almond hidden within. The person who found the almond got to make a wish, or was believed to get married the coming year. After the Christmas Eve feast, someone dressed up as *Tomte,* the Christmas gnome. According to myth, he lived on a farm, or in the forest, and was believed to protect the farmer's home and children from misfortune. *Tomte* resembled Santa Claus and handed out presents while doing funny rhymes. Over the years the Swedes decided to leave *Tomte* in their homeland and adopted St. Nickolas.

On Christmas morning, Swedes attended *Jul Otta*, the traditional church service. Worship, held partly in candlelight, started before sunrise at 5 or 6 a.m. Hymns such as *"Hosiaana,"* which means glory or praise, and *"Var Halsad Skona Morgonstund,"* which means be greeted holy morning time, rang throughout the church. According to Swedish legend, the dead attend *Jul Otta* before the living arrive, and leave grains of dust from their graves on the pews.

December 26th, St. Stephen's Day, was to honor the patron saint of animals, *Staffen*. The tradition on this day was to give the farm animals extra food.

The holiday season continued until *Tjugondag Knut,* St. Knut's Day, on January 13, the day appointed to take down the Christmas tree and decorations. This tradition began in the 11th century by King Knut, who was later canonized by the Catholic church for his kindness and generosity.

During the holiday season, kitchens still bustle with preparations of delicious meals. One meaty dish, *rullsylta,* is made from choice pork back-strap cut in thin layers. Lean beef strips and ten strips of fat are wrapped in layers, cured in a salt brine, and broiled. How do you eat it? Slice and eat with mustard.

Lutefisk, which dates back to the Vikings, took three weeks to make. Preparations started on December 9, the Day of Tuna, in order for it to be ready in time for the Christmas Eve dinner. First of all, the fish (cod) was dried as hard as leather and then buried in ashes. Several days before Christmas, the fish was soaked in a lye solution to rehydrate. The finished product was tender and flaky and served with boiled potatoes. A cream sauce, added as a garnish along with lots of salt and pepper, made a delightful dish. It is believed that early Swedish immigrates brought *lutefisk* on the ships when they came to America, and that was what they ate for the three month's journey. Today the fish is served during ethnic and religious events and is linked with hardship and courage. Also, thanks to local seafood counters, preparation doesn't take three weeks.

Baked breads and cookies grace every Swedish tabletop during the holidays. *Lussekatter,* a Swedish brown bread (sweetened rye bread), and *knackebrod,* a large round, dark, and crisp bread, heads the list of Christmas favorites. Traditionally at Christmas, Swedes hold a *kaffekalas, a* tea party, or rather coffee time, after the meal. Breads, cakes, and cookies, including *spritz* and p*epperkakor,* are served with the coffee. Many Swedes preferred to drink their coffee by pouring it in a saucer, blowing on it, and lapping it up from the rim.

A *smorgasbord* is a type of Scandinavian meal served buffet-style. The word "*smorgasbord*" derives from two Swedish words, "*smorgas*" meaning sandwich, and "*bord*" meaning table. However the table of food ends up being much more than the fixings for a sandwich. They are typically a holiday or celebratory feast, at which time family and guests can help themselves to whatever dishes strike their fancy.

The traditional Swedish *smorgasbord* consists of both hot and cold dishes. It is customary to begin the meal with cold fish entrées such as herring or salmon. Next would be other cold dishes and then hot foods such as Swedish meatballs and other specialties. Dessert was rice pudding sprinkled with cinnamon and sugar.

In the mid 1950s members of the Brushy Free Church decided to have a new organ for their sanctuary. Since funds were not available for the purchase, Reverend Arthur Anderson and his wife suggested a smorgasbord as a fundraiser. Tickets were sold, and guests from Georgetown, Round Rock, Elgin, and Austin attended.

During this time, the church was still located in the country, southeast of Georgetown. The event was held in the summer so that the parsonage lawn, as well as the fellowship hall (the former Bell School House) could be used to seat guests. All of the church members worked to their capacity for this occasion. An organ, on loan from the retailer, was played while guests enjoyed the food, the view, and the breeze. This became an annual event until the church moved into town.

The menu consisted of pickled herring, cheeses, deviled eggs, Swedish brown bread, butter, Jell-O salads, watermelon/fruit salads (carving the rind into a bowl), Swedish meatballs, ham, and chicken, potatoes, and a variety of other vegetables. Desserts were *ostaka,* prune whip and Swedish *spritz* cookies. The most popular drinks were homemade root beer, *drika,* and coffee. The meal and drinks were provided by all of the church ladies. The youth would serve drink refills to the guests. All of the workers wore small white aprons.

The root beer had to be made ten days before serving. Gallons and gallons were made for the occasion. One had to be careful when opening the gallon jars because they could explode, which was a sticky mess to clean up.

Since the majority of the Brushy Evangelical Free Church members were farmers, it's no surprise that they would have an annual Harvest

Festival. In fact, for the first seventy-five years of the church's founding, the worshipers actually held the celebration on Thanksgiving night.

A special program such as guest speakers and/or musicians and singers were invited to participate. During the service when it was time to collect the offering, the men would go to the alter and place their tithe, earned from selling their crops, in the collection plate. The money received that evening was the church's main income for the coming year. After the service, coffee and a variety of pies were served.

When the church moved to Georgetown, the Harvest Festival was held on Thursday evening prior to Thanksgiving for many years. Still, a special program was held and a special offering was taken. Nowadays, the church does not have to rely on one-night's income from the Harvest Festival to make ends-meet. Today, the tithe helps supports mission projects which the church sponsors, and the congregation will have pie and coffee after the service.

Recipes from Swedish Kitchens

Free Church Family Pie

Ingredients:
1 handful of forgiveness
1 pound of unselfishness
1 heaping cupful of love

Directions:
Mix all ingredients smoothly together with complete faith in God. Add 2 tablespoons of wisdom and 1 teaspoon of good nature for flavor. This family pie may be eaten for any occasion, and it any time of day. And since it does not have any calories, one can indulge all one wants.

Joy Nord

Swedish Table Prayer

I Jesu till Bords vi ga
Valsingna Gud den Mat vi fa;
Dit Namn till ara, oss till gagn
So far vi Mat i Jesu Namn.

Appetizers

Appetizer Meat Balls

1 pound lean ground beef
1 teaspoon salt
1/4 teaspoon pepper
1/4 cup catsup
1 tablespoon Worcestershire sauce
1/4 cup finely chopped onion
1/2 cup corn flake crumbs
1/2 cup evaporated milk

Combine all ingredients and mix well. Use approximately 1 teaspoon of meat mixture to shape into a tiny ball. Place in a 13x9 inch baking dish. Bake at 400 degrees for 12 to 15 minutes or until brown. Insert a toothpick into each ball. Serve with barbecue sauce. Yield: 3 dozen balls

Irene Lindquist (1920-2010)

Swedish Nuts

1 cups pecans halves
1 cups walnut halves
1 cup whole almonds
1 cup cashew halves
dash of salt
2 egg whites
1 cup sugar
1/2 cup butter

Toast nuts in a 325 degree oven until brown. Add sugar and salt into egg whites; beat until stiff peaks form. Fold nuts into the egg mixture. Melt butter in a 10x10x1 inch jelly roll pan. Spread nut mixture over butter. Bake at 325 degrees for 30 minutes, stirring every 10 minutes or until nuts are coated with a brown cover and no butter remains in pan. Yield: 4 cups

Naomi Nord (1903-1988)

Easy Black Bean Dip

1-15 oz. can black beans, drained and rinsed
1 teaspoon ground cumin
1/4 teaspoon red pepper flakes (optional)
1/2 teaspoon salt
1 clove garlic, chopped
1 tablespoon lemon or lime juice
1/3 cup chopped fresh cilantro
1-4 oz. can diced green chilies
1/4 cup water, optional

In the bowl of a food processor fitted with a metal blade, puree all ingredients except for water. Add water as necessary if too thick. Taste and adjust seasonings. Serve at room temperature with tortilla chips. Makes about 2 cups.

Betty Ward

Fruit Dip

1 cup pineapple juice
1/4 cup cornstarch
3 tablespoons sugar
2 eggs, slightly beaten
Small container of Cool Whip

Mix the first four ingredients and cook on low-medium heat until thick. Let cool, then add 1 cup of Cool Whip. Serve with various sliced fruits.

Iris Curtis

Salmon Log

1 (15-1/2 ounce) can pink salmon
1 (8 ounce) package cream cheese, softened
1 tablespoon lemon juice
2 teaspoons grated onion
1/4 teaspoon salt
1/4 teaspoon liquid smoke
3/4 cup chopped pecans
3 tablespoons minced parsley

Drain salmon, and remove skin and bones. Flake salmon with a fork. Add cream cheese, lemon juice, onion, salt, and liquid smoke. Stir well. Chill mixture several hours or overnight. Shape salmon mixture into a log. Combine pecans and parsley. Stir well. Roll salmon log in pecan mixture, and chill several hours. Makes one 10 inch log. Serve with celery sticks or crackers.

Letra Nord Avery

Deviled Eggs

6 boiled eggs
2 tablespoons Miracle Whip
1/4 teaspoon salt
2 teaspoons sugar
1-1/2 teaspoons mustard
1-1/2 teaspoons vinegar

Cut eggs in half lengthwise. Remove yolks, leaving whites in halves. Mix yolks with the rest of ingredients. Then fill the whites with the mixture.

Joy Nord

Bean Dip

1 package Philadelphia cream cheese
1 can refried beans
1 12-16 ounce package of shredded Mexican blend cheese
1 medium size jar of Pace chunky salsa

In a microwave safe bowl spread cream cheese, evenly. Then spread a layer of beans, layer of salsa, and top with shredded cheese. Put in microwave, or oven, and heat thoroughly until cheese is melted. Serve with chips.

Letra Nord Avery

Breads

Sourdough Biscuits

1 pkg. dry yeast
1 cup warm water
6 cups self-rising flour
1/2 cup sugar
1/2 cup shortening
2 cups sour milk (or buttermilk)

Dissolve yeast in warm water. Mix dry ingredients together; cut in shortening. Add milk and yeast; mix. Cover and refrigerate until cold. Roll out on floured surface; cut. Place on ungreased cookie sheet. Bake for 15 minutes at 450 degrees F.

Betty Ward

Swedish Oatmeal Bread

2 cups scalded milk
1/3 cup shortening
2 packages yeast
2 cups quick oats
1-1/2 teaspoon salt
1/4 cup brown sugar
1/2 cup warm water
6 cups white flour

Combine milk, shortening, salt brown sugar. Cool to lukewarm. Add yeast, which has been dissolved in warm water, and beat well. Add oats and flour. Mix well and knead 10 minutes. Place in a buttered bowl to rise. Punch /down and let rest for 10 minutes. Shape into 2 loaves and let rise. Bake at 350 degrees for 1 hour or until there is a hollow sound when tapped.

Naomi Nord (1903-1988)

Molasses Wheat Bread

1/4 cup honey
1/4 cup molasses
2 packages yeast
2/3 cup powdered milk (dry)
1 teaspoon salt
2 eggs beaten
1 cup gluten flour
2 tablespoons oil
1/2 cup quick cook oats
1/2 cup wheat germ
1/2 cup whole bran cereal
2 cups whole wheat flour
1-3/4 cups warm water
2-1/2 to 3-1/4 cups white flour

Combine honey, molasses and yeast with the warm water. Let stand until foamy (10 minutes). Stir in milk, eggs, oil and salt. Blend in oats, wheat germ and cereal. Beat in whole wheat and gluten flours. Stir in enough white flour to make a stiff dough. Knead on floured surface from 5 to 8 minutes. Cover and let rise until doubled. Punch down and let rest 10 minutes. Divide into three loaves, place in three pans, cover and let rise until doubled. Bake at 350 degrees for 20 to 30 minutes

Limpa
Swedish Rye Bread

1 package dry yeast
1 teaspoon sugar
1/2 cup water, warm

2 cups beer, heated to lukewarm
2 tablespoons butter, melted
2 tablespoons orange peel

2 teaspoons salt
1 teaspoon cardamom, ground
1 tablespoon caraway seeds, crushed
1/2 cup honey
2-1/2 cups rye flour
3 cups unbleached flour

Dissolve yeast and sugar in the water in a large bowl and proof (foam) for five minutes. Combine beer, honey, butter, and salt. Stir well. Add to the yeast mixture. Add spices. Mix the flours, then add three cups of this mixture to the liquid and beat briskly. Cover with a tea towel, and let rise in a warm, dark place for about an hour. Stir down and add enough of the remaining flour to make the dough stiff but still sticky. Turn out onto a well-floured surface and work the dough until it is smooth and elastic. Add more flour to the surface as needed. The dough will not lose its tackiness completely, but will smooth out a lot. Shape into a ball, grease the dough, and place in a greased bowl. Once again, cover with a tea towel and let rise for about one hour. Punch down, shape into two balls, and put on a greased baking sheet sprinkled with cornmeal. Brush with melted butter, cover loosely with waxed paper, and refrigerate for three hours. Remove from the fridge and let sit uncovered about fifteen minutes. Bake at 375 degrees for 40-45 minutes. Yield 2 loaves.

Swedish Brown Bread

2 cups lukewarm water
1 teaspoon sugar
1/2 package dry Fleischman's yeast
1 teaspoon salt
1-1/2 cups flour
4 tablespoons shortening, melted
3 tablespoons sugar
1/2 to 3/4 cup Grandma's molasses
Extra flour for stiffening

Mix water, sugar and yeast. Let sit a few minutes until yeast is dissolved. Add flour (enough to make a sponge). Cover, let rise in warm place for one hour. Then add shortening, sugar and salt. After mixing well, add molasses to dough, and mix again. Add more flour to make dough stiff. Knead thoroughly. Cover and let rise in a warm place for approximately one hour. Knead a second time and then place in a greased loaf pans. Let dough rise until doubled in size. Bake at 350 degrees for 45 minutes.

Anna Nord (1909-1994)

Ragmunkar

Swedish Potato Pancakes

3 cups grated raw potatoes
1/2 cup milk
1 egg, slightly beaten
2 tablespoons flour
1-1/2 teaspoons salt
1 tablespoon onion, finely chopped

Beat egg into the milk and immediately add potatoes. Sprinkle in flour, mixing well and add salt and onion. Fry in greased skillet, like regular pancakes, until golden brown.

Plattar

Swedish Pancakes

1 cup all-purpose flour
1 cup milk
3 tablespoons sour cream
lingon berry preserves or apple sauce
4 eggs separated
1/2 teaspoon salt

Beat egg yolks until thick. Sift together flour, salt and sugar. Add to yolks alternately with milk. Stir in sour cream. Beat egg whites until stiff. Fold into batter. Heat Swedish pancake pan and butter each depression. Pour about a tablespoon of batter into each depression and spread out evenly. Brown on one side, turn and brown on the other side. Serve hot with preserves or applesauce.

Swedish Sour Cream Waffles

1 cup sour cream
2 eggs
1/2 cup sugar
2 cups water
2-1/2 cups flour
1/2 teaspoons baking soda
1 teaspoon baking powder
6 tablespoons melted butter

Whip cream with egg yolks and sugar. Add water alternately with sifted dry ingredients. Add butter and fold in egg whites. Bake in a hot waffle iron.

Letra Nord Avery

Lussekatter

St. Lucia Buns

2 packages active dry yeast
3/4 cup sugar
1/2 cup butter, softened
1 teaspoon salt
1/2 teaspoon powdered saffron

(dissolved in 2 teaspoons of milk)
1/2 cup dark raisins, if desired
1 cup milk, scalded
6 cups flour
2 eggs
1 teaspoon ground cardamom
1/2 cup blanched almonds, ground
3/4 cup lukewarm water

Soften yeast in lukewarm water. Dissolve thoroughly and add milk and sugar. Beat in 2 cups flour until mixture is smooth. Add butter, eggs, salt, raisins, almonds, cardamom and saffron. Mix well. Add remaining flour and knead until dough is smooth and elastic. Place dough in greased bowl, cover and let rise 1 ½ hours. Punch down and let rise again for 30 to 40 minutes. Shape into various Lucia bun forms and let rise for another 15 to 20 minutes. Bake at 350 degrees for 10 to 12 minutes. Makes 30 to 40 buns.

Yam Muffins

1-3/4 cups all purpose flour
1/2 cup chopped pecans
1/4 cup firmly packed brown sugar
1 tablespoon baking powder
2 teaspoons ground cinnamon
1 teaspoon salt
2 eggs, beaten
1-1/2 cups mashed yams
3/4 cup milk
1/4 cup butter, melted

Combine dry ingredients, make a well in center. Combine wet ingredients, mix well. Add to dry ingredients, stir just until moistened. Spoon into greased muffin tins, filling 2/3 full; sprinkle with cinnamon sugar and white sugar. Bake at 425 degrees for 35 minutes.

Gingerbread

1/2 cup shortening
1/2 cup sugar
1 egg, beaten
2-1/2 cups flour
1 cup molasses
1-1/2 teaspoons soda
1/2 teaspoon salt
1 teaspoon cinnamon
1 teaspoon ginger
1 teaspoon cloves
1 cup hot water

Cream shortening and sugar, then add egg, molasses and dry ingredients. Add hot water last and beat until smooth. This batter is thin. Fold into a greased shallow pan and bake in a 375 degree oven for about 35 minutes.

Rulltarta

Jelly Roll

1/2 cup flour
1 teaspoon baking powder
1/2 cup sugar
1/4 teaspoon salt
1 tablespoon milk
1 teaspoon lemon extract
2 eggs

Separate the egg yolks from the whites. Beat yolks until thick and lemon colored, gradually adding ¼ cup sugar, milk and lemon extract. Beat egg whites until almost stiff; gradually add the remaining sugar. Beat until very stiff. Fold yolks into whites. Combine flour, baking powder and salt; sift three times. Add to egg mixture and fold in. Place on a greased and wax-paper lined 10x15 jelly-roll pan. Bake at 375 degrees for 12 minutes. Loosen sides and turn out onto a towel sprinkled with powdered sugar. Pull off wax-paper. Quickly roll with fresh sheet of wax-paper or sugared towel. Cool. Unroll and spread with jelly, or your favorite filling such as a thick cooked lemon pudding, and then re-roll.

Anna Nord (1909-1994)

Kardemumma Kranz
Swedish Christmas Wreath

1 package dry yeast	1 large egg
1/4 cup water, warm	1/2 teaspoon salt
2-1/2 cups warm milk	1-1/2 teaspoons cardamom, ground
3/4 cup butter, melted and cooled	8 cups all-purpose flour
red and green candied cherries, halved	1 cup sugar

In a large bowl, sprinkle yeast over water and let stand for about five minutes to soften. Stir in milk, butter, egg, salt, sugar, and cardamom until blended. With a spoon, stir in seven cups of the flour or enough to form a stiff dough. Knead dough for about ten minutes or until smooth and elastic. Add more flour as needed to prevent dough from sticking to surface. Place dough in greased bowl, grease top, cover and let rise in a warm place until almost doubled (about 1 ½ to 2 hours). Punch dough down and knead briefly on floured surface to release air. Divide into six equal portions. Pull each into a rope about 24 inches long. Place three ropes on a greased baking sheet, pinch one-end together and braid loosely. Form braid into a ring, pinching both ends together. Repeat to make a second braided wreath. Cover with a tea towel and let rise until almost doubled (about 40 minutes). Bake at 350 degrees for 35-40 minutes, or until loaves are medium brown. Place loaves on rack and let cool 10 minutes before serving.

Lemon icing:

2 cups powdered sugar
1/4 cup milk
1 teaspoon lemon extract

Mix all ingredients. Spoon half of the icing on each wreath, letting it drip down the sides. Decorate with cherries.

Anna Nord (1909-1994)

Coffee Cake

1 cup milk, scalded
3/8 cup butter
1/2 cup sugar
1 teaspoon salt
2 eggs, beaten
3 cups flour
1 package Fleischman's yeast
1/2 cup raisins, optional

Add butter, sugar and salt to scalded milk. Cool until lukewarm. Dissolve yeast in one tablespoon water. Add beaten eggs and yeast to mixture. Add flour and mix well. Let rise, work down with a spoon. Place in greased round cake pan or cookie sheet and let rise until double in size. You can also roll dough to ½ inch thick and spread with brown sugar, cinnamon and a little melted butter, and then shape in a wreath. Bake at 350 degrees for 30-40 minutes. Ice with a powdered sugar glaze. At Christmas time, decorate with red and green candied cherries.

Naomi Nord (1903-1988)

Jast Kranz
Yeast Wreath

Step 1

1 package yeast
3 tablespoons sugar
3 egg yolks
1 cup warm milk
4 cups flour
1 teaspoon salt
1 cup butter

Dissolve yeast, sugar and ½ cup warm milk together, set aside. Beat together egg yolks and ½ cup warm milk, set aside. Mix together flour, salt and butter (this will be like a pie crust). Add the yeast and egg yolk mixtures and mix well. Set in a cool place overnight.

Step 2

3 egg whites, stiffly beaten
1/2 cup sugar
1/2 cup each: nuts, dates, or raisins, if desired
1 teaspoon cinnamon

In the morning, divide into two portions and roll out thin. Mix egg whites with sugar and cinnamon and spread on top of the dough. Sprinkle with nuts, dates, or raisins. Roll lengthwise and shape in a ring. Let rise one hour or until doubled. Bake at 350 degrees for 20 minutes.

Step 3

Frost with ¾ cup powdered sugar blended with cream.

Florence Nord Bowman (1904-2000)

Skorpor
Swedish Rusks

1 cup sugar	1/2 teaspoon soda
1/2 cup shortening	1/2 teaspoon salt
1 egg	1 teaspoon baking powder
1 cup sour cream	1 cup nuts
3 to 4 cups flour (enough to make dough stiff)	

Mix all ingredients and pour onto a long sheet pan. Bake 1 hour at 325 degrees. Take out of oven and turn oven to 200 degrees. Then cut *skorpor* into strips about 1 x 4 inches while still in the pan and put back in the oven to dry until hard and light brown (about 1 hour). These are great coffee-dunkers.

Kringler
Scandinavian Coffeecake

Part 1	Part 2	Frosting:
1 cup flour	1 cup water	1 cup powdered sugar
1/2 cup butter	1/2 cup butter	1 tablespoon butter
1 tablespoon water	1 cup flour	1/2 teaspoon almond extract
	3 eggs	little cream
	1/2 teaspoon almond extract	
		slivered almonds

Mix the ingredients of part one like a pie crust. Put on cookie sheet in 2 long strips 3 inches wide. From the part two list, place water and butter in a sauce pan and heat to boiling point. Stir in flour and mix until smooth. Stir in one egg at a time, beating well after each. Add almond extract. Spread over first mixture. Bake at 400 degrees for 25 minutes.

Frosting: Mix all ingredients. Cool coffeecake just to the point where frosting melts a little when put on.

Frieda Ryden, Rosenblad Familja Cookbook

Swedish Kringler

2 cups flour
1 cup butter
3 eggs
1 cup water
2 tablespoons cold water
1/2 teaspoons almond extract

Mix 1 cup flour, ½ cup butter and 2 tablespoons of cold water into a pie crust. Put in a 9x13 inch pan and pat to ¼ inch thick. Place 1 cup of water and ½ cup of butter in a sauce pan and let come to a boil. Remove from heat and add 1 cup flour and beat till it globs, then add eggs, one at a time beating well after each. Add almond extract. Spread over pie crust mixture and bake at 350 degrees for 55 to 60 minutes.

Frosting

1 cup powdered sugar
1/2 teaspoon almond extract
1 tablespoon butter

Mix all ingredients. Cool cake to a temperature where the icing melts a little when poured on.

Karen Ecklund

Swedish Toast

1 cup butter
2 cups sugar
2 teaspoons baking powder
1 cup chopped almonds
2 teaspoons cardamom seed, crushed
2 eggs
3-1/2 cups flour
1/2 teaspoon salt
1 cup cultured sour cream

Mix all ingredients together like a cake and pour in a 9x13 inch buttered pan. Bake at 350 degrees for 40-50 minutes. When cool, cut into 3 strips across the pan and then cut each strip in half. Wrap each piece in foil and freeze. Remove from freezer as you need them and cut into thin slices and lay singly on cookie sheet. Dry in a 275 degrees oven until thoroughly crisp, turning so they brown evenly.

Marilyn Rosenblad, Rosenblad Familja Cookbook

Rosettes

2 eggs
1 tablespoon sugar
1/4 teaspoon salt
shortening for frying
1 teaspoon vanilla
1 cup milk
1 cup flour
powdered sugar

Mix sugar, salt, vanilla, milk and flour. Beat until smooth. Beat eggs slightly and add to first mixture. For best results, fry in a deep kettle about five inches around and at least four inches deep. Heat oil and then place rosette iron in the oil to heat. Dip iron in batter, but be careful not to let batter cover the upper edges. Immerse n hot oil and keep the iron down until the edges seem golden brown. This will not require more than 20-30 seconds. Remove from oil, tipping iron to drain excess oil and tap iron to remove rosette. Drain on paper towels. Sprinkle with powdered sugar before serving. Yield 35 rosettes.

Allen Rosenblad, Rosenblad Familja Cookbook

Cookies

Pepparkakor

Ginger Snaps

1 cup sugar
1 teaspoon vinegar added to 1 teaspoon soda
1 cup lard
1 teaspoon of each: cloves, cinnamon, all spice, ginger
1 cup dark molasses
2 eggs
4 cups flour

Mix all ingredients. Taking a small amount of dough, knead in enough flour to roll dough out. Cut into round, star or other shape cookies. Place on a non-greased cookie sheet. Bake at 350 degrees for 8 to 10 minutes, watch closely as they easily burn. Yield 6-7 dozen cookies.

Thelma Borg (1914-1996)

Pepparkakor

Mom's Ginger Cookies

6 cups flour
1 cup white sugar
1 cup brown sugar
1-1/2 cups butter
2 eggs
2/3 cup molasses
2 teaspoons cinnamon
1 teaspoon ginger
4 teaspoons baking soda
2 teaspoons cloves
1/2 teaspoons salt

Sift dry ingredients together. Cream sugars and butter, blend in eggs, add molasses, and combine with dry mixture. Roll out on a board and cut with cookie cutter or roll into balls and coat with sugar. Bake at 350 degrees for 8 to 10 minutes. Top with pecans before baking if desired. Makes 92 cookies.

Doris Lindholm

Molasses Sugar Cookies

3/4 cup shortening
1/4 cup molasses
2 cups sifted all purpose flour
1/2 teaspoon cloves
1 teaspoon cinnamon
1 cup sugar
1 egg
2 teaspoons baking powder
1/2 teaspoon ginger
1/2 teaspoon salt

Melt shortening in a sauce pan over low heat. Remove from heat and cool. Then add sugar, molasses and egg. Beat well. Sift together flour, baking powder, cloves, ginger, cinnamon and salt. Add to the first mixture. Mix well. Form into one inch balls. Roll in granulated sugar and place on a greased cookie sheet two inches apart. Bake at 300 degrees for 10 minutes or until lightly browned. Yield 4 dozen cookies.

Lillian Nord Vardaman (1909-2006)

Spritsar
Swedish Spritz

2 cups sifted all-purpose flour
3/4 cup sugar
2 egg yolks
1 cup butter
1 teaspoon almond extract

Sift together flour and sugar. Make a well in center of mixture and add egg yolks, butter and extract. Mix into a smooth dough with fingers. Force through a cookie press onto a non-greased cookie sheet. Bake at 375 degrees for 8 to 10 minutes. Yield 8 dozen cookies.

Swedish Spritz Cookies

1 cup butter
1/2 cup sugar
1 egg
1/2 teaspoon almond extract
2 cups sifted flour

Cream butter and sugar, then add unbeaten egg and almond extract. Add flour and mix well. Place dough into a cookie press using the spritz disk, or any disk of your choice. Press shapes onto a greased baking sheet. Bake at 450 degrees for about 8 minutes. Yield: 6 dozen cookies.

Anna Nord (1909-1994)

Peanut Butter Sticks

12 slices of bread
1/2 cup smooth peanut butter
1/2 Wesson oil graham cracker crumbs

De-crust bread slices, and cut in strips about ¾ inch wide. Place on a cookie sheet and then in a 250 degree oven to dry. Blend together peanut butter and oil until smooth. Dip bread sticks in mixture; let as much drip off as possible. Then roll in graham cracker crumbs. These will keep in air-tight cans indefinitely. Yield about 45 strips.

Thelma Borg (1914-1996)

Kookie Cookies

1 package (9 3/4 ounce) original small Fritos
1-1/2 cups light corn syrup
1-1/2 cups sugar
1-1/2 cups creamy peanut butter

Spread Fritos onto a greased 15 x 10 inch pan. In a saucepan over medium heat, bring syrup and sugar to a rolling boil. Remove from heat, stir in peanut butter until smooth. Pour over Fritos. Cool. Break/cut into squares. Makes about 3 dozen. Store in airtight container.

Angie Cassens

Swedish Brown Sugar Cookies

1 cup firmly packed brown sugar
1 cup dark syrup

1 cup butter
3 eggs well beaten
2 tablespoons thick cream
4-1/2 cups flour
1/2 teaspoon ginger
2 teaspoons baking powder
3 teaspoons cinnamon
3/4 teaspoon nutmeg
3/4 teaspoon cloves

Bring brown sugar, syrup and butter to a boil. Cook for five minutes and then cool well.

Add eggs and cream. Sift together flour, baking powder and spices. Combine with sugar mixture and mix well. Chill or let dough stand overnight. Roll out and cut with cookie cutter. Bake on a greased cookie sheet at 400 degrees for 8 to 10 minutes.

Will Parrot

Brown Swedish Cookies

1/2 cup butter
1/2 cup sugar
3/4 teaspoon honey
3/4 cup flour
1/2 teaspoon baking soda

Preheat oven to 300 degrees. Cream butter, sugar, and honey until well blended. Add flour and baking soda. Mix well. Roll dough into balls approximately one inch wide and then place on a cookie sheet. Use the bottom of a glass dipped in sugar to flatten the dough balls. Bake cookies for 10 minutes or until browned. Allow to slightly cool on cookie sheet before placing on a rack to fully cool.

Crystal Hively

Sugar Cookies

1/2 cup shortening
3/4 cup sugar
1-3/4 cups flour, sifted
1/4 teaspoon salt
3/4 teaspoon cream of tarter
3/2 teaspoon soda
1 tablespoon milk
1 egg
1/2 teaspoon almond extract

Mix together shortening and sugar. Add egg and extract. Sift together cream of tartar, soda, salt, and flour. Mix with milk. Add to the liquid mixture. Roll into small balls and place 3 inches apart on a cookie sheet. Flatten with fork that has been dipped in flour, making a crisscross. Bake at 400 degrees for 8 to 10 minutes. Yield 3 dozen.

Lillian Nord Vardaman (1909-2006)

Coconut Macaroons

3 eggs
2-1/3 cups shredded coconut
1 cup sugar
1 teaspoon vanilla extract

Beat the egg whites until stiff. Stir in one cup of sugar. Put this in a soup plate and set over a kettle of boiling water for 8 minutes until crust forms around edge. Remove and stir in 2 1/3 cups shredded coconut and vanilla. Drop by teaspoon onto a buttered pan and bake in a slow oven.

Florence Bowman (1904-2000)

Smorbakelser

Swedish Butter Cookies

1 cup butter
2 egg yolks
1/2 cup sugar
2 cups flour
1 teaspoon almond extract
1 teaspoon vanilla extract

Blend butter, sugar, egg yolks, and extracts until light and fluffy. Add flour and mix well. Dough will be soft, but not sticky. Roll out on a lightly floured surface and then cut with cookie cutter, or use in a cookie press. Bake at 400 degrees for 8 to 10 minutes.

Snowball Cookies

1 cup soft butter
1/2 cup powdered sugar
1 tsp. vanilla
2-1/4 cups flour
1/8 teaspoon salt
3/4 cup finely chopped nuts

Cream together butter, sugar and vanilla. Add flour, salt and nuts. Chill dough. Roll into 1 inch balls. Place on ungreased cookie sheet. Bake at 400 degrees F. oven 10-12 minutes or until set. Cookies do not spread. While warm, roll in sifted powdered sugar. Cool. Roll in powdered sugar again. Makes 4 dozen cookies.

Betty Ward

Desserts

Prune Whip

12 egg whites
12 large prunes
12 tablespoons sugar
1 teaspoon vanilla
1/4 teaspoon almond extract
pinch of salt

Cook prunes until tender. Remove seeds and cut into small pieces or mash them. Use large bowl to whip egg whites. Add sugar gradually as you start beating on beat speed, and then add prunes and flavorings. Keep beating till very stiff. Bake in a large bowl or casserole dish. Place a pan of water under the dish. Do not preheat oven—place prune whip in oven and then heat at 250 degrees. Bake for 1 hour and then turn oven off. Let prune whip sit in oven for a while. It will rise up, but fall to the original level. Serve with whipped cream or cool whip.

Loraine Ekdahl (1907-1999)

Prune Whip

12 egg whites
dash of salt
12 tablespoons sugar
12 cooked, chopped fine prunes
1 teaspoon cream of tartar
1 teaspoon vanilla or almond extract

Beat egg whites with salt until frothy. Add cream of tartar and beat until stiff peaks form. Don't under beat. Fold in sugar, extract and prunes. Mix thoroughly. Pour in dish or pan and then place in a larger pan with some cold water just so that it floats. Place in cold oven and then bake at 325 degrees for 1 hour or until brown. When done, take pan out of water and let cool. Serve with whipped cream and cherries on top. If you want to make a larger prune whip, use 20 egg whites, 20 tablespoons of sugar, 20 prunes, 2 teaspoons extract, and 2 teaspoons cream of tartar. Bake 1 ½ hours or until brown on top.

Elenora Rosenblad (1903-1971)

Ostaka

(Cheese Cake)

1 gallon fresh whole milk
½ rennet tablet
2 tablespoons water
1 cup flour
1 ½ cups sugar
½ teaspoon salt
4 or 5 eggs, well beaten
½ cup cream

Dissolve flour in a small amount of milk. Then add to the gallon of warm milk. Add dissolved rennet tablet. Stir the mix for 30 seconds. Set in a warm place for one hour until set. Drain off all whey except for about one cup. Add sugar, salt, eggs, and cream. Bake about 1 hour at 350 degrees. When baked, garnish with butter and sugar.

Anna Nord (1909-1994)

Forlorad Ostaka

Cheese Cake

1 quart milk
1/2 cup flour
1 cup sugar
1-2 teaspoons almond extract
2 eggs, slightly beaten
pinch salt
1/4 rennet tablet

Dissolve rennet tablet in a small amount of lukewarm water. Heat milk to just lukewarm. Mix sugar, flour and salt. Pour milk over sugar mixture. Stir in eggs, extract, and rennet mixture. Beat well. Set in hot oven until mixture curdles. Remove from oven and stir mixture. Then pour ½ to ¾ cup whipping cream over top of pudding. Return to oven and continue baking at 325 degrees until done and slightly browned. Serve warm or cold with preserves.

Natalie Johnson Pasco, Rosenblad Familja Cookbook

Cottage Cheesecake

(An imitation to Swedish cheesecake)

1 lb. (16 oz.) cottage cheese (large curd)
2 1/2 cups milk
1/2 c sugar
1/2 c flour (not packed)
1/4 teaspoon almond flavor
3/4 teaspoon vanilla flavor
3 eggs

Mix cheese, 1/2 c of milk, sugar and flavor into baking dish. Beat eggs and flour, add remainder of milk. Heat, but do not boil. Pour over cheese mixture and stir easy. Bake in approx. 400-degree oven for 45 minutes or until brown on top.

Alice Koch

Smalandskostkaka
Swedish Cottage Cheese Cake

16 ounce container, large curd cottage cheese
2-1/2 cups milk
1/2 cup sugar
1/2 cup flour (not packed)
1 teaspoons almond extract
3 eggs

Mix cheese, ½ cup milk, sugar, and almond extract in baking dish. Beat eggs and flour, add remainder of milk. Heat, but do not boil. Pour over cheese mixture and stir easy. Bake at 400 degrees for 45 minutes or until brown on top.

Grace Koch

Great Grandma Carter's Pecan Pie

1 cup dark Karo syrup
3 small or 2 large eggs, slightly beaten
1 cup sugar
1-8or 9 inch pie crust
2 tablespoons margarine or butter
1 teaspoon vanilla
1 cup pecans (add last)

Mix the first six ingredients, then pour into pie crust. Bake at 350 degrees until pecans are slightly brown and custard is set. About 45 to 50 minutes.

Iris Curtis

Peanut Butter Pie

1 prepared pie crust
1 (8 ounce) package cream cheese, softened
1 cup creamy peanut butter
1 cup sugar
1 tablespoon butter
1 teaspoon vanilla
1 cup heavy cream, whipped

Mix cream cheese, peanut butter, sugar, butter, and vanilla until smooth. Fold in whipping cream. Garnish with grated chocolate.

Appelpudding

Apple Crisp

1 cup sugar
1 cup sifted all purpose flour
1 teaspoon double action baking powder
1/2 cup butter
6 medium size cooking apples
1 cup cold water
plain or whipping cream

Mix together sugar, flour and baking powder. Cut in butter until mixture resembles corn meal. Pare and core apples. Slice into an 8x8 inch baking pan. Sprinkle with flour mixture. Pour water carefully over all. Bake at 275 degrees for 50 to 60 minutes. Serve warm with plain or whipped cream. Yield 6 to 8 servings.

American Daughters of Sweden Cookbook

Frozen Banana Dessert

1 small can crushed pineapple (drained)
8 ounce cool whip
1 cup buttermilk chopped nuts & cherries (optional)
3 bananas (mashed)
1 cup sugar

Mix all ingredients together and put in freezer. Dessert will keep up to six weeks.

Natalie Johnson Pasco, Rosenblad Familja Cookbook

Applesauce Cake

2-1/2 cups flour
2 cups sugar
1/4 teaspoon baking powder
1-1/2 teaspoons soda
1-1/2 teaspoons salt

2 eggs
1/2cup water

3/4 teaspoon cinnamon
1/2 teaspoon cloves
1/2 teaspoon allspice
1/2 cup shortening
1-1/2 cups unsweetened applesauce
1 cup raisins
1/2 cup walnuts (optional)

Grease and flour cake pan(s). Blend dry ingredients in a bowl. Add shortening, water and applesauce. Beat 2 minutes on medium speed. Add eggs and beat 2 more minutes. Stir in walnuts, raisins and spices. Pour into pans. Bake-layers 35 to 40 minutes or oblong 45 to 50 minutes. Tastes best warm and without icing.

Lillian Nord Vardaman (1909-2006)

Chocolate Dream Cake

Cake

2 cups flour
2 cups sugar
1/2 cup (1 stick) margarine
1/2 cup shortening
1 cup water
1/4 cup cocoa
1/2 cup buttermilk
2 eggs, slightly beaten
1 teaspoon soda
1 teaspoon vanilla
1 teaspoon cinnamon (optional)

Sift flour and sugar into mixing bowl; blend well. In a sauce pan bring margarine, shortening, water and cocoa to a rapid boil. Pour over flour-sugar mixture and mix well. Combine remaining ingredients and add all at once to batter. Mix well. Pour into a greased, lightly-floured 13x9 inch pan. Bake at 400 degrees for 35 to 40 minutes or until it tests done. Let cool 10 to 15 minutes while preparing frosting.

Dream Frosting

1/2 cup margarine
3-1/2 tablespoons cocoa
1 pound powdered sugar
1/3 cup milk
2/3 cup chopped pecans
1 teaspoon vanilla

Combine margarine, cocoa and milk in a saucepan. Heat slowly and bring to a boil. Add remaining ingredients. Beat well and spread over cake while still warm. Leave cake in pan until ready to serve. Cut in squares.

Grace Koch

Perfect Butter Cake

1 cup butter
1 ½ cups sugar
3 cups flour
1 ¼ cups sweet milk
½ teaspoon vanilla
½ teaspoon lemon extract
3 teaspoons baking powder
5 egg whites

Cream butter and sugar, then add milk and flavors. Sift flour with baking powder about 4 times. Beat egg whites until stiff and mix in last. Pour into greased and floured pan(s). Bake at 350 degrees for 30 minutes. Ice cake layers with favorite frosting.

Florence Nord Bowman (1904-2000)

Swedish Nut Cake

Cake

2 cups sugar
2 eggs, slightly beaten
20 ounce can undrained, crushed pineapple
1/2 cup walnuts or pecans, chopped
2 teaspoons baking soda
2 cups flour
1 teaspoon vanilla

Mix together all ingredients. Pour into a 13x9 inch pan. Bake at 350 degrees for 35 minutes or until it tests done.

Topping

8 ounce cream cheese, softened
1-3/4 cups powdered sugar
1/2 cup walnuts or pecans, chopped
4 ounces butter
1 teaspoon vanilla

Mix together all ingredients and beat with a beater. Spread on hot cake.

First Christian Church Cookbook

Risgrynskaka
Swedish Rice Porridge

3 cups milk
salt
1 cup rice
3/4 cup sugar
cinnamon

Place milk in the top of double boiler. Add salt to taste. Add rice and cook until thick. When thick add sugar. Stir well. If it is too thick, add some cream or milk. When cooked pour into a dish. Sprinkle cinnamon on top.

Anna Nord (1909-1994)

Swedish Pudding

3 eggs, well beaten
1 cup flour
1 cup sugar
½ teaspoon baking powder
1 cup chopped nuts
1 cup chopped dates

Mix all ingredients. Bake at 325 degrees for one hour. Let cool and serve with whipped cream.

Marian R. Powers, Rosenblad Familja Cookbook

Toscas

Swedish Almond Tarts

Crust

6 tablespoons butter, room temperature

1/4 cup sugar
1 cup all-purpose flour

Filling

1/3 cup almonds, slivered
1/4 cup brown sugar
2 tablespoons butter
1-1/2 tablespoons cream
2 teaspoons all-purpose flour

To make crust, cream butter with the sugar in a mixing bowl. Mix in flour and stir to make a smooth dough. Divide the mixture by placing even amounts into the cups of a twelve-cup muffin tin. Press the mixture into the bottom and up the sides of each cup.

To make filling, mix the almonds, brown sugar, and butter in a small pan. Stir in the cream and flour. Cook and stir the mixture constantly over medium heat until it boils (about 10 minutes). Divide the mixture evenly between the prepared tart shells.

Bake at 350 degrees for 10 to 15 minutes or until tops and crust are light brown. Cool at least 15 minutes before removing tarts from pan, and then cool completely on a rack.

Great Grandma Dodge's Blackberry Bread Pudding

2-1/2 cups self-rising flour
1-1/2 cups sugar
2 large or 3 small eggs
1 tablespoon vanilla
1 cup milk
1/3 cup cooking oil
2 cups blackberries

Mix all ingredients except blackberries into a batter; do not make batter too thin. Fold blackberries into batter. DO NOT STIR. It will make the batter dark. Pour into a greased and floured casserole dish. Bake at 350 degrees for 35 to 40 minutes or until golden brown.

Iris Curtis

Bread Pudding

1/2 loaf bread cubed
3 cups milk
1 cup sugar
2 eggs
1/2 teaspoon vanilla
1/4 cup shortening
1/2 teaspoon cinnamon
1/8 teaspoon baking soda
1/2 cup raisins
salt

Place cut up bread in a large bowl. Pour milk over bread and let stand. Cream shortening and sugar. Beat in egg yolks. Dissolve soda in 1 teaspoon of water, and then add along with a dash of salt and vanilla. Fold in egg whites. Mix well. Add to bread mixture. Mix well, again, and then pour in baking dish. Bake at 350 degrees from 40 to 60 minutes. Place a pan of water under the baking dish while baking.

Note: You can add a can of fruit cocktail, or pecans. Also you can substitute the three cups of milk by using 1 cup of coffee and 2 cups of milk. This is an extra treat for those coffee lovers, and it changes the whole taste of the pudding.

Lemon sauce (for pudding)

2/3 cup sugar
1-1/4 tablespoons cornstarch
1-1/4 cups boiling water
1-1/2 tablespoons lemon juice
1/8 teaspoon nutmeg
grated rind of 2 lemons

In a sauce pan, mix sugar and cornstarch together. Add water gradually, stirring constantly, boil for 5 minutes. Remove from heat and add the remaining ingredients. Stir until thick. Pour over bread pudding on each serving.

Lillian Nord Vardaman (1909-2006)

Drinks

Dricka

Homemade Root Beer

1 bottle root beer extract
5 gallons lukewarm water
4 pounds sugar
1/2 cake fresh compressed yeast

Dissolve yeast in a cup of lukewarm water. Add other ingredients. Stir well. Bottle immediately and place in a warm location for two days. Serve in three or four days.

Anna Nord (1909-1994)

Strawberry Cream Slush

1 cup frozen or fresh strawberries, sliced
1 cup crushed ice
1/4 cup milk or cream
2 Tablespoons sugar
3 drops red food coloring (optional)

Place strawberries, ice, cream and sugar into blender. Blend until slushy. Add food coloring and blend 5 seconds longer.

Aleah Curtis

Wassail

2 quarts apple juice or cider
1 pint cranberry juice
1 small orange spiked with whole cloves
1 teaspoon aromatic bitters
2 sticks cinnamon
3/4 cup sugar

Place all ingredients into a crock pot. Cover and cook on high for one hour. Reduce heat to low and simmer 4 to 8 hours. Serve warm. Makes 12 cups.

Meats, Main Dishes

Potatiskorv
Potato Sausage

6 large raw potatoes (peeled and ground)
1-1/2 pounds ground beef
2-1/2 pounds ground pork
1 medium onion (ground)
1 cup milk
1 teaspoon pepper
2 teaspoons salt
1 teaspoon allspice

Mix all ingredients together and stuff into sausage casings (be careful not to overfill as they will expand while cooking). Prick casing several times with a needle before cooking. Put into a pot of hot water and boil over medium heat for 1 hour. Then brown in a frying pan. Makes six 24-inch sausages.

Sausage Squares

1 pound pork sausage, cooked, crumbled; drain
1 cup (4 oz.) shredded cheddar cheese
1 cup (4 oz.) shredded Monterey Jack cheese
1/2 cup finely chopped onion
1 can (4 oz.) chopped green chilies
1 tablespoon minced jalapeno pepper
10 eggs
1 teaspoon chili powder
1 teaspoon ground cumin
1/2 teaspoon garlic powder
1/2 teaspoon pepper

Place cooked and crumbled sausage in greased (or lined with foil) 13 in. by 9 in. by 2 in. baking dish or pan. Layer with cheeses, onion, chilies, and jalapeno. In a bowl, beat eggs and seasonings. Pour over other ingredients in dish. Bake, uncovered, at 375 degrees for 18-22 minutes or until a knife inserted near the center comes out clean. Cool for 10 minutes; cut into 1 in. squares. Yield: about 8 dozen.

Betty Ward

BBQ Meatballs

3 pounds of frozen meatballs
2 cups ketchup
1 cup brown sugar
1-1/2 teaspoons liquid smoke
1/2 teaspoon garlic powder
1/4 cup chopped onions

Place frozen meatballs in slow cooker. Mix together the rest of ingredients and pour over the meatballs. Cook on low for 6 to 9 hours.

Becky Overstreet

Kottbullar
Meatballs

2-3 slices bread
1 egg, beaten
1 pound ground beef
1/2 pound ground pork
1/2 pound ground veal
1 cup milk
1 onion, grated
1/2 teaspoon pepper
1/2 teaspoon ground allspice
butter

Mix well and then form into small balls. Brown in butter. Place in baking pan and bake at 350 degrees for 30-35 minutes.

Rosenblad Familja Cookbook

Meat Balls

1 pound ground meat
1 small onion, chopped
1/2 cup tomato juice
1/2 cup cracker crumbs
1 teaspoon pepper
1 teaspoon salt
About a 1/2 cup flour

Mix all ingredients and then form into small balls. Roll in flour. Place in a well greased baking dish that has been lined with cracker crumbs.

Sauce

1/2 cup catsup
1 cup No. 2 whole tomatoes
1 teaspoon dry mustard
1 teaspoon salt
3 teaspoons lemon juice
1 teaspoon vinegar
1 teaspoon sugar
1 teaspoon pepper

Mix all ingredients together and then pour over meat balls. Bake at 350 degrees for 45 minutes.

Lillian Nord Vardaman (1909-2006)

Swedish Beef Roast

5 pound beef or rump roast
2 teaspoons salt
1 tablespoon vinegar
1 cup water
15 each peppercorns
1 onion, chopped
1 bay leaf
1 tablespoon brown sugar
1 tablespoon whiskey
1 tablespoon butter

Melt butter in a Dutch oven and brown meat on all sides. Add the remaining ingredients. Cover tightly and cook slowly for 2 ½ to 3 hours, or until meat is tender. The pan juice can be made into gravy by adding ½ cup of cream. Serves 6 adults.

Betty Turkette

2 cups macaroni, cooked & drained
3 cups turkey, cooked
1 cup diced ham
1/4 cup minced pimento
1 can cream of mushroom soup
1 cup chicken broth
1/2 cup onion, grated
1-1/2 cups sharp American cheese
salt and pepper to taste

Mix all ingredients except ½ cup grated cheese together. Season with salt and pepper to taste. Pour into a 1 ½ quart baking dish. Sprinkle top with remaining cheese. Bake at 350 degrees for 45 minutes.

Lillian Nord Vardaman (1909-2006)

No Work Chicken

Chicken breast (5 or 6)
1/2 cup honey
1/2 cup wet mustard
1 tablespoon curry powder
2 tablespoons soy sauce

Place chicken snugly, skin side down, in a baking dish in one layer. Make marinade by mixing together honey, mustard, curry powder and soy sauce. Pour over chicken and refrigerate six hours or overnight. When ready turn chicken, cover dish with foil and bake at 350 degrees for 1 hour. Remove foil, baste well, and continue baking uncovered for 15 more minutes. When serving, spoon sauce over chicken.

Olive Rosentrater (died 2006)

Pecan Chicken Quiche

Crust	Filling	
1 cup all purpose flour	3 eggs	1/4 cup minced onion
1 cup shredded sharp cheddar cheese	1 (8 ounce) sour cream	1/4 teaspoon dill weed
3/4 cup chopped pecans	1/4 cup Miracle Whip	3 drops hot sauce
1/2 teaspoon salt	1/2 cup chicken broth	1/4 cup pecan halves
1/4 teaspoon paprika	2 cups cooked chopped chicken	
1/3 cup vegetable oil	1/2 cup shredded cheddar cheese	

Combine first five crust ingredients, stir in oil. Set 1/4 of mixture aside for topping. Press remaining mixture into bottom and sides of 9 inch quiche pan. Prick with fork and bake at 350 degrees for 10 minutes. Set aside. Combine eggs, sour cream, Miracle Whip, and chicken broth in medium bowl. Stir well. Stir in cheese, chicken, minced onion, dill and hot sauce. Pour mixture in crust. Sprinkle with rest of flour mixture on top and garnish with pecan halves. Bake at 325 degrees for 45 minutes or until knife comes out clean.

Swedish Ham Balls

2 pounds ground ham
1 pound ground pork sausage
2 cups soft bread crumbs
2 eggs, well beaten
1 cup milk

1 cup brown sugar
1 teaspoon dry mustard
1/2 cup vinegar
1/2 cup water

Mix ham, sausage, bread crumbs, eggs and milk. Form into small balls and place in baking pan. In a sauce pan, combine sugar, mustard, vinegar and water. Bring to a boil and stir until sugar is dissolved. Pour over balls. Bake at 325 degrees for 1 hour. Baste frequently.

Rhoda Ann Lind, Rosenblas Familja Cookbook

Baked Salmon Patty

1 (15-1/2 ounce) can salmon, de-boned
1 cup bread crumbs
1/2 cup milk

2 eggs, beaten
1 tablespoon parsley
1 tablespoon lemon juice

1/4 teaspoon pepper
1 tablespoon butter

Mix all ingredients and press into a greased baking pan. Bake at 350 degrees for 45 minutes.

Lillian's Texas Hash

1-1/2 pounds ground beef
1-1/2 cans tomato sauce
1 cup uncooked rice
1/2 onion, diced
1/2 bell pepper, diced
1/2 teaspoon salt
1/2 teaspoon pepper
1/2 teaspoon garlic salt
1/2 thyme
1/2 teaspoon sweet basil

Brown ground beef in skillet. Add onion and bell pepper. Stir well. Add the rest of ingredients and cover and let simmer for about 45 minutes. Stir occasionally.

Lillian Nord Vardaman (1909-2006)

Agg Rorra

Egg gravy

2 tablespoons bacon or sausage drippings
4 cups milk
2 tablespoons flour
2 egg yolks (slightly beaten)
1/8 teaspoon salt

In a skillet over medium heat, put meat drippings. Add flour. Blend and let brown a bit. Mix milk, egg yolks and salt. Add to flour and mix until thick, but do not allow it to curdle. Add more milk for thinner gravy. When mixture is the right consistency for your taste, remove from heat and serve with Swedish rye bread or biscuits.

Lutefisk

First purchase dried *lutefisk*, sometimes called stockfish. Using a hacksaw, saw it in 6 inch pieces. Some people remove the skin before soaking, by pulling it off with a pair of pliers. Then soak the fish in clear water for 3 days, change the water every day. On the 4th, 5th, and 6th day soak in ashes (preferably ashes from live oak wood). The ashes should be placed in a cloth bag, and placed in the water with the fish. If the ashes are not available you can soak the fish in lye water using a teaspoon of lye per gallon of water, changing to a clean solution every day. This takes care of the 4th, 5th, and 6th days. On the 7th day, 8th, and 9th days, soak in clear water, changing water every 12 hours. After the 9th day it should be ready to eat. If you didn't skin the fish before you started, do so on the 9th day. The pieces of fish should be about 2 inches thick and the meat white and pretty.

When using lye if the fish seems to be getting slimy, cut down on the lye or use your own judgment and soak it in lye for only 2 days.

To Cook: Place fish in a large pot, cover with water and bring to a boil for 20 minutes with pot covered. The aroma fills the house and even your Swedish neighbors know what you're cooking. When the fish has finished cooking, drain off water. Take the fish out of pot, debone it, place flakes of beautiful white fish on platter. Cover it with your favorite cream sauce and sprinkle pepper on top. Serve the fish with boiled Irish potatoes, cranberries and homemade brown bread and homemade root beer. For your guests that don't like the smell of the fish, give them a decorated clothespin to put on their nose!

Emory Carlson
Swedish Heritage Cookbook

Lutefisk with White Sauce

1 pound lutefisk or cod fish, flaked into pieces
2 cups milk
2 tablespoons flour
2 tablespoons butter
salt and pepper to taste

Combine milk and flour in a sauce pan. Cook over a medium heat until boiling. However, use a whisk to stir mixture constantly to prevent lumps and so it does not scorch. Add salt and pepper to taste plus butter. If the sauce is too thick, add more milk. Slowly mix in fish and cook until well heated. Serve over boiled white potatoes.

Angie Nord Cassens

Kallops

Swedish stew

Beef ribs are good cut in pieces. Roll in flour and brown in some fat. Then season with salt and pepper. Add a bay leaf. Bake or cook very slowly. When nearly done place two carrots with meat and add some water to prevent from burning.

Kaldolmar

Swedish Cabbage Rolls

1 egg
2/3 cup milk
1/4 cup onion, chopped fine
1 teaspoon salt
dash pepper
1 teaspoon Worcestershire sauce
1/2 pound lean ground beef
1/2 pound reduced fat ground pork
3/4 cup cooked rice
6 large cabbage leaves
1 tablespoon lemon juice
1 tablespoon brown sugar
1 (8 ounce) can tomato sauce or 1 (10-1/2 ounce) can condensed tomato soup

In a large bowl combine egg, milk, onion, salt and pepper. Mix well. Add beef, pork, rice, and Worcestershire sauce. Mix together well. Immerse cabbage leaves into boiling water for 3 minutes, or until limp; drain. The heavy vein in center of cabbage leaf may be trimmed a little for easier rolling. Place ½ cup of meat filling onto each cabbage leaf. Fold in sides and roll over meat. Place rolls in a baking dish. Blend tomato sauce (or tomato soup), brown sugar, and lemon juice. Pour over cabbage rolls. Bake at 350 degrees for 1 ¼ hours. Baste twice with sauce.

Meshy Malouf

Cabbage rolls

½ cup rice
1 pound ground beef
salt and pepper
1 medium head cabbage
3 lemons
garlic

Cook rice and mix with meat. Soften cabbage leaves by dipping in boiling water for one minute. Roll ingredients in leaves and place in a large pot with a few buttons of garlic in between the layers of rolls. Lay loose leaves of cabbage on top of rolls. Cover with water and simmer for 30 minutes. When done, squeeze juice from lemons over rolls.

Catfish Delight

3 or 4 catfish filets
1 large cream cheese (8 ounce)
1 teaspoon Dijon mustard
1 teaspoon lemon juice
1 tablespoon horseradish
4 slices bacon
1 onion chopped
salt and pepper

Place catfish in baking dish. Salt and pepper. In a mixing bowl blend cream cheese, mustard, horseradish, and lemon juice. In a fry pan, fry bacon until crisp. Set aside. In bacon grease, sauté onion. Crumble in bacon. Then pour into the cream cheese mixture and blend until smooth. Spoon over fish till it cannot be seen. Bake at 350 degrees for 30 minutes or until light brown on top.

Lillian Nord Vardaman (1909-2006)

Sausage Balls

1 pound sausage
1 cup shredded cheese
1 cup Bisquick

Mix with hands. Bake at 325 degrees for 30 minutes.

Smothered Okra

1 pound cut up okra
1 can tomato paste
1 pound sausage, cut in1inch pieces
onion

Brown okra in skillet, add onion, paste plus 3 cans of water. Stir well. Add sausage. Cook for 20 to 30 minutes.

Soups, Salads, Vegetables

Frukt Soppa

Fruit soup

1 package dried mixed fruits
12 ounce package dried apricots, chopped
3 tablespoons quick cooking tapioca
1 cup raisins
1 cup prunes, chopped
1-1/4 cups sugar

Add fruits to two quarts of water. Stir in sugar and bring to a boil. Cover and simmer over low heat for 20-25 minutes or until fruits are fork tender. Add tapioca and let stand until thickened in covered pot. Serve hot or cold. Makes 10-12 one cup servings.

Allene Rosenblad, Rosenblad Familja Cookbook

Swedish Fruit Soup

1 cup prunes
1 cup apricots
1/2 cup raisins
1 cup sugar
2 apples cut in pieces
2 or 3 slices pineapple cut in pieces
1/2 cup tapioca
2 cinnamon sticks
1 cup orange juice
1/2 cup pineapple juice
Juice of 1 lemon
1 quart boiling water

Boil prunes and apricots until nearly done. Then add other ingredients and boil until done or when soup begins to thicken. Serve hot or cold, as a cocktail or dessert.

Marion Johnson

Inlagd Gurka

Cucumber salad

1 pound cucumber
1-1/4 cups water
1/2 cup Swedish spirit vinegar (or distilled white vinegar)
1 cup sugar
finely chopped parsley

Cut cucumbers into thin crosswise slices. Mix the vinegar, water and sugar together. Set aside for a few minutes, stirring occasionally until sugar is dissolved. Pour the dressing over the cucumbers and add a generous sprinkling of parsley. Chill for at least two hours before serving. Also chopped onions can be added to this recipe and Splenda may be used as a sugar substitute.

Enid Anderson Olson

Corn Pudding

2 cans cream corn
2 eggs, beaten
1/2 cup sugar
1/2 cup milk butter

Mix all ingredients together and place in a greased baking dish. Dot with butter. Bake at 350 degrees for 1 hour or until set.

Florence Nord Bowman (1904-2000)

Cauliflower and Broccoli Salad

2-1/2 cups chopped broccoli
2-1/2 cups chopped cauliflower
1 cup red onion
2/3 cup Miracle Whip
1/3 cup buttermilk
2 teaspoons celery seed

Combine vegetables in a large bowl. Add remaining ingredients, toss well. Chill.

Lillian's Cantaloupe Salad

1 medium cantaloupe
1/2 cup pineapple cubes
1/2 cup mayonnaise
1/3 cup French dressing
lettuce
1/2 cup diced bananas
1/2 cup sliced strawberries
1/2 cup diced orange
lemon

Chill all fruits. Just before serving, cut cantaloupe into quarters, peel and scoop out seeds. Squeeze on a dash of fresh lemon juice. Arrange cantaloupe on salad plates, garnish with lettuce. Combine fruit and French dressing. Mix lightly. Pile fruit on cantaloupe quarters. Top with mayonnaise. Honey dew melon may be substituted for cantaloupe. If so, sprinkle on a dash of lime juice instead of lemon juice.

Lillian Nord Vardaman (1909-2006)

Green Vegetable Salad

1 (16 oz.) can French style green beans, drained
1 (16 oz.) can peas, drained
1 (8 oz.) can lima beans, drained
1 small onion cut into rings
1/2 cup chopped green pepper
1/2 cup salad oil
3/4 cup sugar
1 teaspoon salt
1/2 cup vinegar
1/2 teaspoon pepper

Combine vegetables and set aside. Combine remaining ingredients, blend well and then stir into vegetables. Cover and refrigerate several hours, stirring occasionally.

Sauerkraut Slaw

1 (16 oz.) can sauerkraut, drained
2 medium stalks celery, cut into pieces
1 small green bell pepper
1/2 cup onion, chopped
1/4 cup sugar
1/3 cup sour cream
1/2 teaspoon celery seed

Chop sauerkraut into short pieces. Add remaining ingredients. Stir well. Cover and refrigerate for 24 hours before serving.

Bruna Bonor

Swedish Brown Beans

1-1/2 cups brown beans
1-1/2 quarts water
1 tablespoon salt
4 tablespoons syrup
1 tablespoon cider vinegar
1 tablespoon cornstarch
1 stick cinnamon

After washing beans, soak them in cold water overnight. Do not pour off water in which beans were soaked. Add salt to water and boil. As soon as beans are nearly done, add syrup, vinegar, and cornstarch. If necessary, add more hot water. Continue cooking until beans are soft.

Natalie Johnson Pasco

Jansson's Temptation

6 medium sized potatoes
2 tablespoons butter
2 medium sized onions, thinly sliced
1 can (3-1/2 ounce size) of Swedish anchovy fillets
2 tablespoons bread crumbs
3 tablespoons butter
3/4 cup cream or half and half
dash of pepper

Peel and cut potatoes into 2x1/4 inch strips, and then store in cold water to prevent discoloration. Melt 2 tablespoons of butter in skillet and add onions; cook until soft but not brown (about five minutes). Pat potatoes dry. Arrange layers of potatoes, onions and anchovies in a greased 1 ½ to 2 quart baking dish. Begin and end with potatoes. Dot top layer of potatoes with butter, add dash of pepper, and bread crumbs. Pour cream around the potatoes. Bake at 400 degrees for 45 to 60 minutes. The potatoes should be tender and most of the liquid absorbed.

Seasoned Green Beans

1 one pound pkg. frozen green beans
1/4 to 1/2 cup chopped onion
1 tsp. powdered beef bouillon
3-4 Tablespoons of water

Microwave in three minute increments, stirring to combine ingredients. Cook until you are satisfied with texture.

Betty Ward

Potatoes Supreme

1 pkg. frozen hash brown potatoes
1 teaspoon salt
1-8ounce jar Cheese Whiz
1 can cream of celery soup
1 cup milk
1 small can chopped green chilies
1 tablespoon minced onion

Put hash browns in a buttered baking dish. Mix together the remaining ingredients and pour over potatoes. Bake at 350 degree for 45 minutes to one hour.

Becky Overstreet

Sue's Veggies'

1 pkg. Normandy vegetables
1 can cream of mushroom soup
1/3 cup sour cream
1 cup shredded Mozzarella cheese
1 cup French fried onion rings

Mix the first 3 ingredients with 1/2 cup cheese and 1/2 cup onion rings. Cover and bake at 350 degrees for 45 minutes. Top with remaining cheese and onion. Bake until brown.

Becky Overstreet

Broccoli and Rice Casserole

1 pound chopped broccoli
4 cups of cooked rice
1-8 ounce jar of Cheese Whiz
1 stick margarine
1 can cream of mushroom soup

Mix ingredients and cook at 350 degrees for 30 minutes. Stir before serving.

Becky Overstreet

Sweet Potato Soufflé

4 cups cooked yams
1 cup sugar
1 egg
1/2 cup milk
1 cup packed brown sugar
1 cup chopped pecans
1/2 cup flour
1 stick butter

Combine first four ingredients. Mix well with an electric mixer. Pour into casserole dish. For topping, melt butter and crumble in other ingredients. Spread over potato mixture. Bake at 350 degrees for 40 minutes.

Doris Lindholm

Onions Au Gratin

2 1/2 cups sliced onions
4 tablespoons butter
2 1/2 cups grated cheddar cheese, divided
1/3 cup packaged biscuit mix
1/4 teaspoon salt
1/8 teaspoon pepper
3 tablespoons butter, melted

Sauté onions in 4 tablespoons of butter until tender. Mix onions with 2 cups grated cheese, biscuit mix, salt, pepper, and melted butter. Pour into greased casserole dish. Sprinkle with remaining 1/2 cup cheese. Bake at 350 degrees for 30 minutes.

Doris Lindholm

Squash Casserole

5 to 6 small yellow squash, washed and sliced
3 eggs, beaten
1/2 cup milk
2 tablespoons butter
6 crackers, crumbled
1 small onion, grated
1 cup cheese, grated
salt and pepper to taste

Boil squash in a small amount of water until tender. Drain. Mix remaining ingredients with squash and put in buttered casserole dish. Top with bread crumbs, if desired. Bake at 350 degrees for 30 minutes.

Doris Lindholm

Zucchini Parmesan

4 cups zucchini, thinly sliced
1 small onion, sliced
1 tablespoon water
2 tablespoons butter
1 teaspoon salt
3 tablespoons grated parmesan cheese
pepper

Put first six ingredients in a skillet. Cover and cook for one minute. Uncover and cook, turning with wide spatula until barely tender, about 5 minutes. Sprinkle with cheese, toss.

Doris Lindholm

Spanish String Beans

2 cans green beans, drained
1 large onion
1 can whole tomatoes
1 green bell pepper, chopped
1 clove garlic
1 cup packed brown sugar
2 tablespoons bacon fat
1/2 cup ketchup

Sauté onion and add the rest of ingredients. Cover and cook for 20 minutes until well heated.

Doris Lindholm

Eggplant Casserole

1 large eggplant, pared and cut into chunks
1 egg, slightly beaten
1 medium onion, chopped
1 stack of saltine crackers, crushed
butter, salt and pepper, to taste
cheddar cheese, grated

Peel and chunk eggplant, then soak in salted water for 30 minutes. Drain salt water, and add fresh water to eggplant. Cook until tender. Drain. Mash eggplant, add egg and onion, stir. Add butter, salt and pepper. Add crushed saltines and stir well. Place in a casserole dish and top with lots of cheese. Bake at 350 degrees for 30 minutes. Can be cooked in a microwave. Yellow squash can be substituted for eggplant.

Doris Lindholm

Footnote: The recipes without a submitted name are from the author's kitchen.

REFERENCES

Swedes in Texas in Words and Pictures, Copyright 1994, New Sweden 88 Austin Area Committee, Publisher J.M. Ojerholm

Historical Round Rock, Copyright 1985, Nortex Press, a Division of Eakin Publication, Inc. Authors Jane Digesualdo and Karen Thompson

Golden Jubilee, Swedish Evangelical Free Church of the U.S.A. 1884-1934

Brush Evangelical Free Church, Golden Jubilee Reminiscence 1891-1941

Sixtieth Anniversary booklet July 3-8, 1951

Seventieth Anniversary booklet, July 5-9, 1961

Ninetieth Anniversary booklet, July 7, 1981

One Hundredth Anniversary Celebration booklet, July 7-14, 1991

Texas Posten, publication number (USPS 541-400) Austin News, July 2, 1981

Deeds Records, Office of the Williamson County Clerk, Georgetown, Williamson County, Texas

Georgetown Evangelical Free Church cemetery records